THE
LAST FILIPI...

HeaD HunterS

DAVID HOWARD

LAST GASP OF SAN FRANCISCO
777 Florida St., San Francisco, CA 94110, Attention: Ron Turner, publisher.

Design: David Howard
www.artexhibitionrentals.com

Published and distributed by
LAST GASP OF SAN FRANCISCO,
777 Florida St., San Francisco, CA 94110
www.lastgasp.com

ISBN 0-86719-507-X

First Printing, March 2001

Printed in Hong Kong

Library of Congress Cataloging-in-Publication Data

Last Gasp
of San Francisco

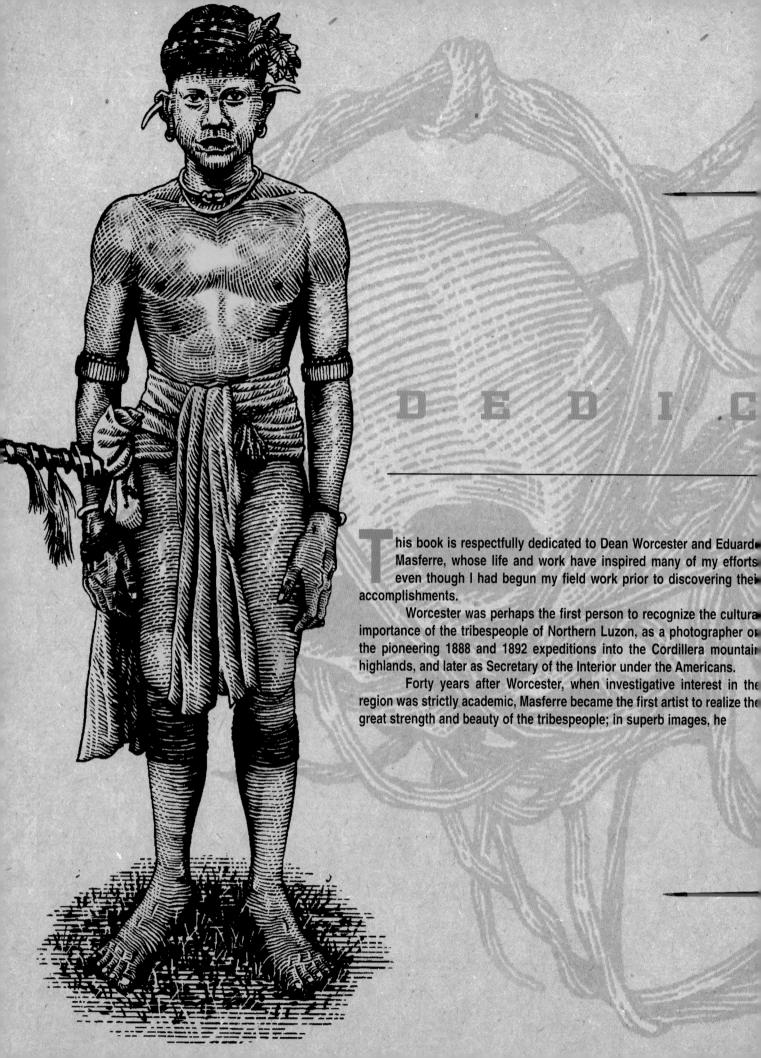

This book is respectfully dedicated to Dean Worcester and Eduardo Masferre, whose life and work have inspired many of my efforts even though I had begun my field work prior to discovering their accomplishments.

Worcester was perhaps the first person to recognize the cultural importance of the tribespeople of Northern Luzon, as a photographer on the pioneering 1888 and 1892 expeditions into the Cordillera mountain highlands, and later as Secretary of the Interior under the Americans.

Forty years after Worcester, when investigative interest in the region was strictly academic, Masferre became the first artist to realize the great strength and beauty of the tribespeople; in superb images, he

David Howard and Eduardo Masferre at Masferre's studio in Sagada, Mountain Province, Philippines, 1994.

A T I O N

Kalinga tree house The Field Museum collection # 24770

ecorded a vanishing way of life for future generations. For more than two decades between 1934 and 1956, Masferre traveled and took photographs in the highlands, although it was not until 1988 that his monograph was finally published.

Forty years after Masferre completed his project, I found myself following in the master's footsteps. I consider myself privileged to have met the photographer in his home, and to have personally contacted the people and the culture he depicted so lovingly in his art.

Finally, this dedication is extended to all the Filipino people, whose fortitude in the face of centuries of foreign occupation and internal oppression is a testament to their courage and independent spirit.

Dean Worcester and an Ifugao guide during the 1892 expedition. American Museum of Natural History collection # 2133.

contents

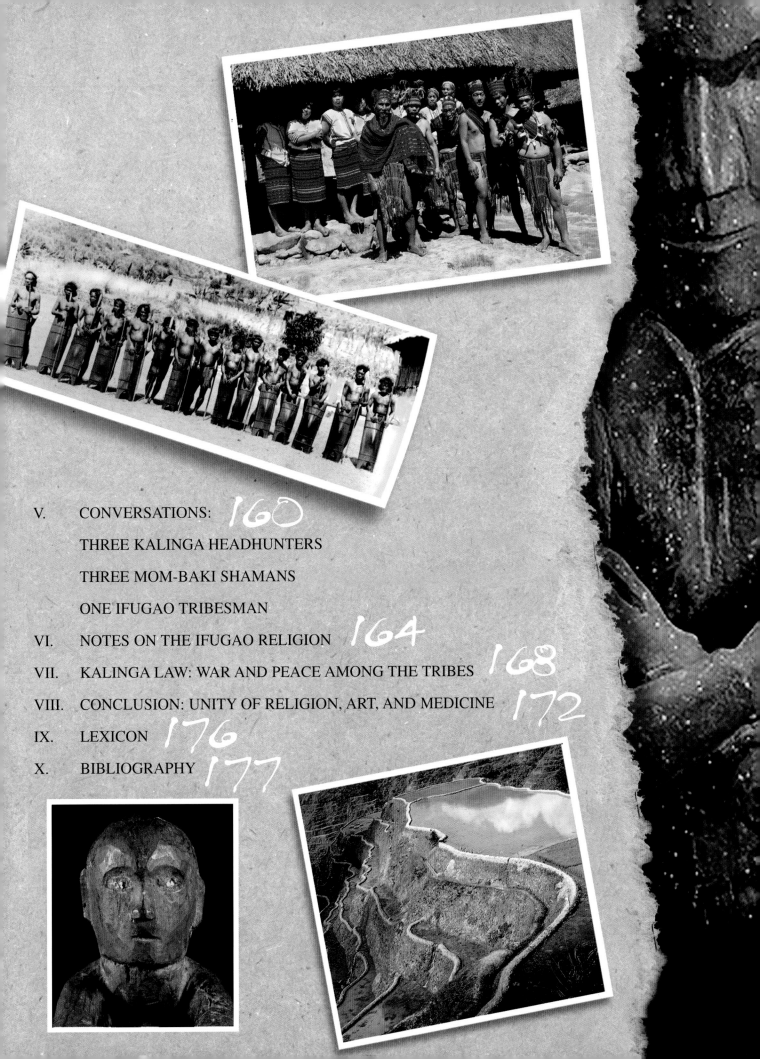

PREFACE

A long series of coincidences and changing circum stances led me to the Philippines, although eve from the beginning, my journey felt more like a ca ing. My rational mind is aware of the impossibility of ar such preordained destiny, but my instinctual se assumes that there is a spiritual direction. The tribe people I met assured me a man's life and work are pa of a larger plan, in which nothing happens by accide or error.

This experience has given me something believe in again— a new set of values and ideals a timeless as the universe. I view art and life differer ly, because I now look to the best qualities of prim tive tribal culture when forming my own aesthet and philosophical criteria.

A few years ago I knew virtually nothing about th Luzon mountain highlands and their indigenou peoples. The Luzon tribes to my mind, were litt more than imaginary relics of some prehistor period, to be relegated to the same dusty she stacked with myths and folktales. During th 1980s, however, I became interested in primitiv art and culture. As a photographer, I found prin itivism a refreshing alternative to the high a culture of museums and galleries, which I ha been immersed in for so many years. Bore and exhausted by the treadmill of exhibitior and openings that had been my life since m first showings two decades earlier, I wa searching for a new mode of expression. first approached primitive art from a collec tor's viewpoint, but my interest in the artifact was integrated with my work as a photogra pher, when I began to visit and photograph th tribes whose artifacts I eventually collected.

I originally had no intention of travelling t the Philippines, but a chance opportunity to vis a friend in Manila brought me to the islands as tourist. I made some sidetrips to the islands c Mindanao and Mindoro, but torrential rains and flooc ing made travel impossible. Returning to Manila, found myself idle with a week remaining before m scheduled departure. I had heard of the Luzon high lands tribespeople, and on a sudden impulse I ven tured to Bontoc in the Mountain Province. The cultur and community I found there seemed to strike a vita missing chord within my artistic and spiritual self.

At every stage of my journey through the world c

ghland villages, I have had the assistance and support of friends, both old and new. Collectors, scholars and students of primitive art and culture have been generous in helping me access useful information and clarifying my personal observations. Many individual Bontoc, Kalinga and Ifugao tribespeople have extended the hand of friendship to me— a list of each one would be impossible. Hopefully, their personalities and stories have been adequately presented in this book.

A word of acknowledgement is due to the many writers, museum curators and researchers who assisted me. Historical photographs and artifacts from many institutional collections were made available, including materials from The Hearst Museum of Anthropology, UCLA's Fowler Museum of Cultural History, The Field Museum in Chicago, The American Museum of Natural History, The Brooklyn Museum, The Metropolitan Museum of Art, The Smithsonian Institution, The Natural History Museum of Los Angeles County, The University of Pennsylvania Museum of Archaeology and Anthropology, The Peabody Museum of Archaeology and Ethnology at Harvard University, The Newark Museum, and the Treganza Museum of Anthropology at San Francisco State University.

Finally, the important contributions of the University of the Philippines, which through its Baguio City campus maintains the highly acclaimed Cordillera Studies Center, deserves recognition here. Its counterpart in Manila, the Centro Escolar (the University Research and Development Center), provided assistance for the ongoing field investigation of the indigenous cultures of the Luzon highlands. The Malacanang Palace Museum in Manila also offered critical analysis and insight for my project. These institutions all deserve the continuing support and funding of government and private agencies, both in the Philippines and abroad.

It is my hope that continuing research and documentation of the fading culture of the tribes of Northern Luzon will achieve what is desperately sought by most of the native informants interviewed in this book: the preservation of the remaining villages, rice terraces and burial grounds of the Ifugao, Bontoc and Kalinga peoples. If the photographs and experiences offered in this book further this purpose, I will feel my efforts have been justified.

The Philippines is a farflung Southeast Asian country, consisting of more than 7,000 islands, on the southwestern fringe of the Pacific Ocean. The islands stretch over nearly 1,800 kilometers of ocean. Only 700 are actually inhabited, and the dozen largest islands contain most of all of the country's habitable land area. The two largest of these islands, Mindanao and Luzon, are home for two-thirds of the nation's population of over 60 million. Northern Luzon's smaller population of primitive tribal groups inhabit remote mountain villages. These tribes, dubbed "cultural minorities," have very little in common with the majority of their Filipino countrymen dwelling in the Southern lowlands.

Settled by seafaring Malayo-Polynesian explorers more than 4,000 years ago, the Philippines were unknown to the West until 1521, when Ferdinand Magellan circumnavigated the globe. European colonization of the Philippines has since been ironically summarized as: "four hundred years in a convent and fifty years in Hollywood," referring to the nearly four centuries of Spanish rule and a subsequent half century of American influence.

Kalinga tribesman from, the village of Bugnay, 1993

Ifugao tribesman from, the village of Poitan, 1994

Ifugao female from Mayayao,
Field Museum # 32408, **circa 1890**

PHILIPPINES

LUZON

BAGUIO

PHILIPPINE SEA

SOUTH CHINA SEA

MANILA

MINDORO

SAMAR

PANAY

SULU SEA

NEGROS

PALAWAN

↑

150 MILES

MINDANAO

CELEBES SEA

Ifugao tribe dressed for ceremonial ritual
Field Museum # 30823, **circa 1890**

The Ifugao village of Batad.

The rice terraces surrounding the Ifugao village of Batad.
(facing page)

Although the dominant influences have been Spanish and American colonial cultures, the natives of the Philippines were even more deeply influenced by earlier contacts with the peoples of India, China, Arabia and the various islands of the South Pacific and Indian Ocean. These mariners first disturbed the isolation of the islands around 1,000 A.D., when they began trading for the Filipinos' abundance of pearls, gold, coral and spices. In exchange, the foreigners brought Chinese, Hindu and Islamic culture and religion to the more settled lowland areas of the islands.

In spite of the Philippines' long history of foreign occupation and domination, the tribes in the interior regions have preserved their culture to a remarkable degree. Throughout the islands, hundreds of distinct ethnic groups still speak at least seventy-seven known indigenous languages, all of the Malayo-Polynesian linguistic family. The dozen largest of the Philippine islands have 26 designated "cultural minorities," nine of which live on Luzon, the northernmost and largest island with over 100,000 square kilometers of land mass. The remote mountain highlands of northern Luzon have long been the strongest pocket of resistance to colonization, and remain one of the last bastions of indigenous culture on the island.

The Kalinga village of Bugnay (above).

Children at home in the village of Batad (right).

American Museum of Natural History collection # 2069, Dean Worcester, photographer (left).

American Museum of Natural History collection # 1729, Dean Worcester, photographer (right).

Bontoc headhunting warrior, The Field Museum # 18636 (below).

The Filipino mainstream underwent a forced conversion to Christianity and many received European or American style educations under the colonial regime. These questionable benefits never reached the more isolated tribes in many of the remote mountain villages. There, the tribes still remain virtually unchanged in their customs and traditions, even well into the late twentieth century.

Although the people of northern Luzon are indigenous to the area and maintain a unique character and culture, ultimately they are descendants of the same mixed population of immigrants who make up the general population. The villages have historically been outcasts from the Filipino urban culture, because of their secluded geographical situation and their misunderstood tribal practices—among which the greatest source of contention was headhunting. The tribes are acutely aware of the slow deterioration of their way of life, while still observing the character and practice of their ancient folk religion, which has always been viewed as pagan and alien by the Christian majority.

The indigenous people in the isolated region, within the Cordillera Mountains, have persisted in their way of life for thousands of years. Three of the tribes: the

Kalinga headhunter warrior with "Pinagas" ax, Field Museum, Chicago, Collection # 24680

Bontoc warrior with "Linglingo" fertility earring. American Museum of Natural History # 2067. Dean Worcester.

Young Ifugao warrior with "linglingo" necklace. American Museum of Natural History # 2151. Dean Worcester.

Kalinga warrior with "O-Kong" hat. Field Museum, Chicago # 26249. All Dean Worcester images circa 1890

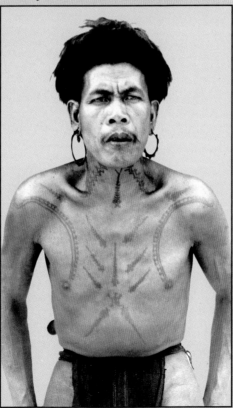

Ifugao headhunter warrior. American Museum of Natural History # 2151. Dean Worcester.

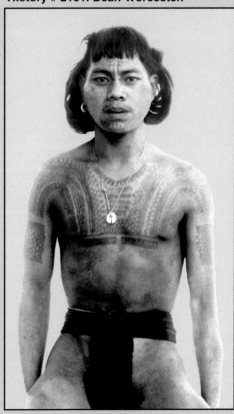

Bontoc headhunter with "Chak-Lang" tattoos. American Museum of Natural History # 2151. Dean Worcester.

Bontoc, Ifugao and Kalinga have among their elders the last living headhunters in the Philippines. Their rituals and shamans have survived more than four thousand years of evolution and struggle, only to now face cultural extinction. The few remaining headhunters can still be encountered and observed, but their culture is rapidly dying out, mainly because Christianity has subverted the ancient tribal values.

Today, only a few of the tribal elders have actually performed all the ancient rituals and practices of the culture. With the demise of these elders, the ancient customs will finally cease to exist. The younger generations have forsaken all but the most superficial characteristics of their native culture, many of them taking on the outer trappings of Western culture. Tragically, an ancient and admirable way of life now seems doomed to extinction unless attention can be drawn to the dignity and value of the culture.

The opportunity to visit and photograph the people of a vanishing culture comes rarely. North from Baguio City, the provincial capital, a traveler can easily undertake a journey into the land of the "Igorots": the now unpopular name given to the collection of tribes in the upland northern territories along the Chico river and the surrounding Cordillera Mountains. The Bontoc, Ifugao, and Kalinga tribes are still practicing their rituals in the villages within the mountains. However it appears the tide has turned, and what was once a stronghold of tribal heritage is fading, succumbing to the weight of five hundred years of Christian influence.

"Mom Batak" Ifugao harvest sacrificial ceremonial ritual (right). The Field Museum, Chicago, collection # A 32263, 32260, 32261.

The Chico river (below).

Lakay Kaibayo, respected elder of "dap-ay" Bilig, wearing a "boaya" ritual necklace; made of boar, dog, and crocodile teeth, strung with woven rattan. Sagada, Mountain Province, 1950, by Eduardo Masferre: David Howard's collection.

The Ifugao village of Cambulo 1994

The Ifugao village of Cambulo 1996

Sagada, Mountain Province 1952 Eduardo Masferre

Kalinga village of Saklit 1950 Eduardo Masferre

The tribes living in and around the periphery of the Cordillera mountain range were the last to be subdued by the incursion of Spanish missionaries and soldiers moving inland, upriver from the Northern Luzon coastline.

In the remote interior of the highlands a natural fortress of rugged mountains and deep ravines prevented the Spanish invaders from completing their conquest of Northern Luzon. For many centuries, three main tribal groups have divided the central Cordillera into contiguous territories, with the Chico River roughly bisecting the region. The Bontoc, Ifugao and Kalinga tribes inhabiting the central Cordillera are only a few generations removed from a completely authentic tribal culture.

The Kalinga village of Bugnay 1996

The Ifugao rice terraces of Banaue 1995

These three groups co-exist as more or less independent tribes, each with their own province and ruling council. The recent political division of the highlands has only reinforced the natural segregation of the tribes. Bontoc is the capital and cultural center of the Bontoc tribe's Mountain Province; Lagawe, to the southeast, is the capital of Ifugao province; and to the north, Tabuk is the capital of Kalinga province.

The inhabitants of these beautiful alpine provinces, can be viewed as one singular group, consisting of three very unique regional cultures. It is no wonder the tribes people have rarely wandered very far from home, vigorously defending their culture, way of life, an their sacred world within the Cordillera Mountain highlands.

In many respects, the story of the highland "Igorots" has been a tale told by European and American researchers, rather than the mountain tribes themselves. Yet we can only become fully-realized individuals by recognizing and accepting other peoples' positive influences, without imposing our own preconceived cultural assumptions and prejudices. In the following records of travels and conversations, twelve tribes people, for the first time, speak as one distinctive voice, with an eloquence and a passionate spirituality, which previously often eluded Western understanding and appreciation.

The Ifugao rice terraces of Banaue 1997

The climate within the Luzon highlands' Grand Cordillera is as varied as its topography, ranging from steamy tropical forests in the lowlands thru the northeast and the southwest, to cool alpine forests at the highest elevations. The central highlands, furrowed by steep ravines and mountain ridges, is watered by fast mountain streams feeding into three main river systems— the Chico, the Syouc and the Asin. Throughout the valleys and along the narrow winding riverbeds, hundreds of villages have existed independently for countless centuries, their cultures protected from contact with the outside world because of the extreme difficulty in travelling to the interior.

The circumstances under which the Cordillera was first inhabited are shrouded by time and myth, but there is little doubt that several major waves of settlement have taken place over the last four thousand years.

A primordial Paleolithic population has alway been hypothesized by anthropologists, but there is no evidence of their passage that might give us a clue to the civilization and its character. Almost as far back in prehistory were the "Negritos," the first people whose descendants can still be found within the isolated Luzon highlands' few remaining tribal groups. The first wave of outside settlement occurred perhaps five thousand years ago, when migrants arrived on the north coast of Luzon and proceeded up the river valleys to the Cordillera mountains. It is believed these "Indonesian Type B" people mixed with the Negritos forming a new racial stock.

Kalinga male with "lufay" fertility pendant 1995

The Kalinga village of Botbot

The Kalinga village of Ambato on the Chico River

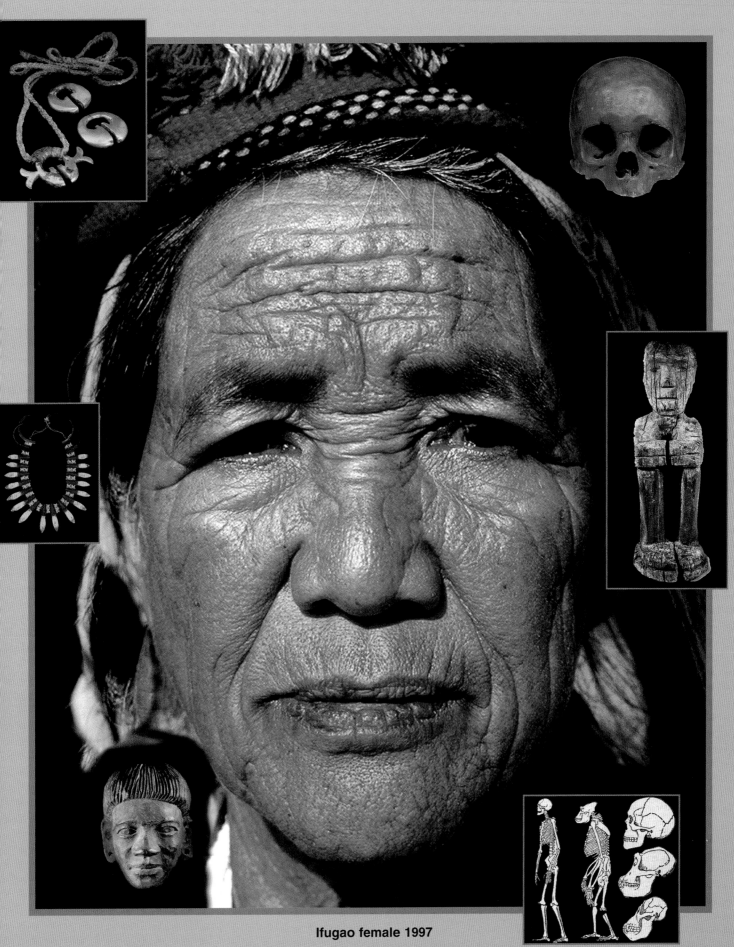

Ifugao female 1997

Ifugao tribesman Batad village 1993 (left)

"Lumatac" Kalinga headhunter from the village of Tulgao with "fatoc" chest tattoo 1994 (above)

The successive wave of Chinese, Indonesian an Malayan migrations account fc the mostly Asian genotypes c today's highlanders, but an add tional factor— the Spanish cor quest— complicates the evolu tionary sequence even furthe Although it seems clear som Filipinos fled to the hills upon th arrival of the Spanish in Manil Bay in 1564, it is far from clea exactly which people or hov many, ultimately assimilated int the tribal mountain population.

The Spanish had little interest i exploring or settling the high lands, but reports of gold an other precious metals in th mountains to the north led t numerous expeditions during th colonial period. The first suc excursion in 1567, brought bac enough gold to justify furthe exploration over the next half century, but the few strikes an poor yields dampened enthusi asm for over three hundre years, until another gol rush took place. Under th Spanish colonial regime, th entire Cordillera region wa known as Benguet province without any tribal or geographi distinctions.

The migrants presumably brought their knowledge of rice cultivation with them, since the first evidence of rice paddies dates from around 2000 B.C. Then some time between about 800 and 500 B.C., another great wave of migration from the same part of East Asia poured over the same area, and extended their stock to the present day areas of the Bontoc, Ifugao, and Kalinga provinces. Finally, around 300 B.C. a Malayan population arrived which provided many of the more advanced arts and crafts forming the basis of the present cultures, including pottery, weaving, metalwork and most importantly, retaining walls and advanced irrigation of the kind found in the magnificent rice terraces.

In spite of abundant evidence suggesting the Cordillera tribes originated, predominantly from the Asian mainland, it seems reasonable to suppose the aboriginal Paleolithic stock more certainly contribute to the Bontoc, Ifugao, and Kalinga tribes.

Kalinga female Luplupa village 1995

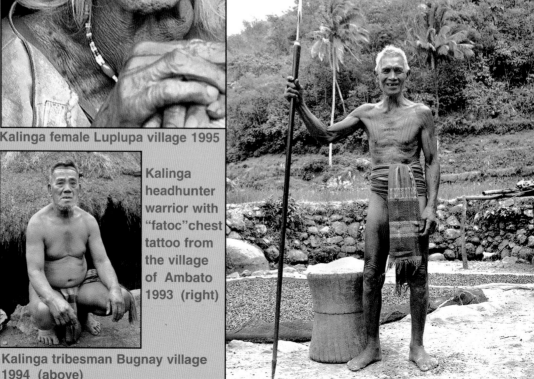

Kalinga headhunter warrior with "fatoc" chest tattoo from the village of Ambato 1993 (right)

Kalinga tribesman Bugnay village 1994 (above)

Ifugao tribesman from Banaue 1993

The unity was in keeping with the monolinguistic character of the region, where all the mountain languages are derived from a single basic structure, and separate tribal and village dialects are believed to have only developed in the modern period. At first, the Spanish seemed to respect the frontiers of this remote region, on the principle that a peaceful relocation of the tribes would be more easily achieved rather than a forced uprooting of the culture. Then in the eighteenth century, the missionaries in the outposts in Apayao and the Abra River Valley began pressing the Spanish authorities to subdue the mountain people, whose pagan ways and alleged violence were corrupting their converts.

The nineteenth century saw the policy of peaceful resettlement of the tribes give way to military force. Although the ostensible reason for this shift was to prevent the mountain people from harming Christian settlements along the periphery of the Cordillera, in fact the motive was less spiritual. The government had established a new tobacco monopoly in 1781, and the mountain people had retaliated by increasing tobacco production, initiating trade which could realize greater profits independently rather than from crops grown under government levies. During the 1830s, punitive expeditions against the Bontoc, Kankanay, Ifugao and Ibaloi tribes were conducted. So great was the devastation that "many large towns that existed...could not be found" when the Americans arrived at the turn of the century. (Ellis, 1981)

It was not until the middle of the nineteenth century that the Spanish finally settled on a policy of divide and conquer, splitting the mountain province of Benguet into smaller administrative regions which could be more effectively governed by military occupation. The Spanish set up heavy fortifications flanking the highlands on the south, west and southeast, and from their stronghold in Abra and Lepanto to the south, they sent out armed parties into the Kalinga and Bontoc territories. Within a few years, the Spanish were able to establish a semi-permanent base at Bontoc, but the tribes proved so hostile that the camp could not be reinforced substantially until the building of a mission in 1892.

The Spanish military campaigns were aimed indiscriminately at the Bontoc, Ifugao and Kalinga tribes, all of whom remained implacably hostile to any occupying forces until the arrival of the Americans. The Ifugao attacked Christian settlements, and the mission in Kiangan actually had to be closed between 1871 and 1889.

Ifugao ritual dance: Field Museum # 22307 circa 1890

Kalinga ritual dance: Field Museum # 32278 circa 1890

Bontoc warriors with "kalasag" shields and "tobi" spears
American Museum of Natural History # 2087, Dean Worcester, photographer

Kalinga tree house: Field Museum # 24770

The town of Bontoc: The American Museum of Natural History # 2110   Dean Worcester photographer 1888-1913

Kalinga warrior with his house: Field Museum # 24772

Bontoc men work the rice terraces: Field Museum # 18611 circa 1890

Bontoc boy and rice granaries: Field Museum # 18664

Ifugao house: Field Museum # 22339

Just two years later, a resident missionary at Kiangan persuaded some Ifugao converts to destroy their Baki religion's "bulul" rice granary idols, causing a serious rift among the villagers. The insensitive and tactless destruction of the native religion convinced many tribes people the Spanish meant to destroy their culture. During more than three hundred years of occupation, the Spanish had failed repeatedly in their efforts to stamp out "paganism" in the mountains, and the conquerors eventually turned their attention to pacifying and settling the lowland regions on the perimeter of the Cordillera. After the American conquest of the islands in 1898, however, the separate identities of the main tribal groups were finally recognized through the creation of three separate tribal districts. This division of the region into autonomous political units was misleading, because each tribe was in reality an informal extended group of villages, centered around linguistic and cultural similarities rather than central ruling bodies or distinct political districts of any kind.

The more subtle local cultural and linguistic variations were recognized later, after anthropologists discovered differences among the tribes. Each group came to be viewed as an individual entity with specific characteristics and customs. The first American field expeditions of 1888 and 1892 had established a distinct province for each tribal group, and more importantly, they produced the invaluable images of Dean Worcester, the expedition's photographer. On the basis of this knowledge, a new system of district governments was established in the Mountain Province, with Bontoc as the capital and local districts governed by councils of elders. The civil authorities continued to push for a program which would bring the headhunting mountain tribes into the mainstream culture of Christian Filipinos.

The effort to convert the tribes, to Christian English-speaking citizens of the newly-Americanized Filipinos, ran afoul because of persistent low-level tribal warfare. The Americans recognized the significant cultural and religious differences between the Bontoc,

Ifugao Bulul rice granary figures

Ifugao headhunting trophy from the village of Hiwag

Ifugao, and Kalinga tribal groups. The Ifugao did no[t] concentrate their numbers in large villages, it wa[s] observed, but preferred remote and inaccessible spot[s] where they could defend their settlements wit[h] only a few warriors. The Kalinga wer[e] regarded, then as now, as the fiercest an[d] most untamed of the tribes, exemplified i[n] the intermittent recurrence of civil strif[e] and internal tribal warfare. The Bonto[c] were recognizably different from th[e] Kalinga and Ifugao, but their "tribe[s]" could be logically subdivided into [a] dozen ethnic groups based on differ[e]nt dialects, agricultural technologie[s] and modes of warfare. Unfortunately pluralism did not fit in very well with th[e] American brand of centralized coloni[al] authority. The initial American respons[e] to the disorganization and lack of trib[al] and political centers in the mountai[n] highlands was to impose a single mili[-] tary-civilian authority, presiding over [a] confusing assortment of districts. B[y] 1906, the American program to con[-] struct trails, organize tribal councils and educate the tribespeople was i[n] full swing. The first step in the progra[m] was to construct a complete system o[f] trails, bridges and ferry boat[s] throughout the accessible area[s] of the highlands.

The second step was t[o] introduce modern communica[-] tions, which meant stringin[g] telegraph and telephone lines u[p] to the mountain towns and build[-] ing roads connecting the norther[n] towns to the south, so wagons[,] automobiles, and buses could tra[-] verse the foothills, allowing busi[-] nessmen access to remote mar[-] kets. In the outlying areas veg[-] etable farming, mining, and log[-] ging operations were established[,] and further economic develop[-] ment in the region was a high pri[-] ority for American policy makers.

Ironically, the America[n] program to facilitate intertriba[l] communication and transporta[-] tion came on the heels of the firs[t] establishment of formal tribal divisions. The new tech[-] nologies brought the tribespeople into closer contac[t] with each other during a period of rapid social and tech[-] nological change. The Americans shared the origina[l] Spanish ambition to "subdue" the mountain tribes, bu[t] lacking a single religious and cultural ideology, the ne[w] "Bureau of Non-Christian Tribes" took the position not to attack or despise the customs, usages and traditions of the locality... Religious practices, usages and customs which are not contrary to law, morals and good customs should be tolerated and respected." Of course headhunting was not among the exotic customs to be countenanced. American bureaucrats attempted to establish schools and health programs, but quickly realized the tribes had their own agendas concerning education and wholesome practices. The early educational administrators soon discovered the people "dislike to have their children go away from home. The boys prefer the free life of the village to the discipline of the school and frequently run away." Public health programs also met with little success, as the Americans found their naive ideas of the highlands in conflict with the reality of unruly autonomous tribes. On the whole, the Americans found the natives friendly but decidedly uncooperative when it came to their assimilation program. In most other respects, the American plan for the development and pacification of the provinces met with more success, exemplified in the completion of a road from the coast to the mountainous interior and the decision to restore Filipino administrative rule by 1916. Spanish speaking Filipino administrators then began to surface and predominate. Centralization, which was an ambitious plan slowed, if not reversed, as new village schools were established throughout the provinces. The first secondary school in the highlands was then established, and the numbers of English speaking, formally educated mountain people grew steadily in the following years. Efforts to modernize the provinces met with setbacks on a regular basis. Shortly after the end of the First World War, for example, a work party of 1,500 Ifugao built a new road to the neighboring province of Nueva Ecija. Beset by smallpox and influenza, the few survivors of the work force returned to their village, spreading the epidemic throughout the province. Cultural conflicts between American and Filipinos escalated further in the 1920s, as lines were drawn between the more aggressive Filipinos favoring national self determination with eventual independence, and the Americans seeking to make the colonial status permanent. During the 1920s and 1930s, the first generation of fully educated tribes people emerged in the Mountain Province. Guided by these enlightened tribal representatives, the

Dean Worcester attending to the burial of an Ifugao headhunting victim
American Museum of Natural History # 2133, circa 1890

Bontoc "anito" headhunting boundary marker: American Museum of Natural History

The grave filled and marked: American Museum of Natural History # 2139, Dean Worcester photographer, circa 1890

American administrators developed a new justice system based on a balance of statute law and tribal custom. This system covered conflicts ranging from the tribal peace pacts; governing headhunting, to a wide range of personal rights and extensive clarification of personal property laws.

Ifugao tribesman from the village of Tam-an 1997

Ifugao female from the village of Tam-an 1997

By the 1930s, roads from all four corners of the provinces to the interior were nearing completion. An extensive school system had been established throughout the region, and a high level of agriculture and light industry had been established.

The decisive force in the push for development was the discovery of mountain gold, 250 miles north of Manila, at Antamok Creek, in 1927. By 1933, at the depth of the Great Depression, scores of mining companies were operating in the highlands. While the rest of the world underwent economic hardship, the Mountain Province experience relative prosperity even though the mining booms crashed regularly. Progress was not without its price, for the invading miners found a region where formal ownership and legal land titles were unknown. The conflicts between miners and natives were not entirely one-sided, as some of the locals

"Gem-o": Ifugao shaman
from Batad village 1993

also had an interest in the mines. A series of events contributed to the collapse of the boom. The first was the fall of the price of gold on world markets in 1934-5, after which gold mining was confined to a few of the more productive sites and some ongoing prospecting in the less explored areas within the Kalinga province. The second focused on the coming of Filipino independence, which would inevitably give greater power to the people of the mountains in their struggle against the invasion of prospectors and missionaries. The third related to several scandals surrounding sales to locals of worthless mining claims, whose duped victims camped out on sites around villages throughout Bontoc, unwilling to accept that they had been swindled. Bontoc was claimed "the common property of the nation"

Kalinga warrior performing the "Lalo" dance ritual in Bontoc 1993

(and hence subject to outside exploitation). The government watched helplessly, while hundreds of armed Bontoc warriors invaded the camps and claims of the prospectors and occupied the treetops and higher ground to defend their homeland. The terrified prospectors called the constabulary, and when they arrived to oversee a settlement they found the province on the brink of open war. The authorities conceded they were unable to deter the natives from their "gallant... effort to defend what they honestly believe to be their heritage (by withstanding) the persistent onward march of industry... and civilization" (Fry, 1983:187). The Bontoc tribe had once again successfully organized and armed themselves against invading forces seeking to despoil their land and culture. Unfortunately, there was little the mountain people could do to resist the Japanese invasion force that swept over the islands in the wake of Pearl Harbor, although the mountains could still provide sanctuary for Filipinos fleeing the conquerors. The American drama of MacArthur's defeat and triumphant return largely by-passed the highlands, where the resistance and Japanese invasions had been infrequent. During the course of the war, however, Northern Luzon was a scene of constant struggle between the resistance and the Japanese imperial army, with considerable casualties from periodic bombing and armed raids in pursuit of the Filipino rebels. The Cordillera once again became a stubborn stronghold of resistance to the foreign invasion of the islands. In a repeat of the region's historic role in the final days of the Spanish-American war, the Luzon highlands became the last hideout of the most obstinate of the occupation forces. It was several years before the last Japanese fugitive came down from the mountain caves and surrendered to the local authorities. The Philippines had finally gained complete independence. Just as it had at the end of the Spanish-American conflict, the unstable transition between ruling powers, had once again brought uncertainty into the lives of the tribes. Now the perceived threat comes not from an invading army of foreigners bent on conquering the country, but rather from a more subtle enemy with a materialistic focus: an invisible Filipino adversary, from within.

Ifugao female 1994

Kalinga male 1993

Kalinga female 1995

Kalinga female in the village of Ambato 1993

Ifugao mother and daughter in Tam-an village 1995

"Lingayan": Ifugao female in the village of Banaue 1993

Kalinga female with a "raincoat" in the village of Ngibat 1994

The latest adversary is the unbridled drive for economic progress and modernization, the ruling elite had thrust upon their own mountain tribes. Against these overwhelming pressures the Bontoc, Ifugao, and Kalinga tribes continue to struggle to maintain their integrity and independence. Today, the tribespeople are still proud and independent, under the protection of the Filipino government, they enjoy the privileges and benefits accorded to the twenty-six officially-designated "cultural minorities" throughout the islands. Paradoxically most of the elders accept this new status and the hope it provides for cultural survival, while successive generations seem eager to cast off tribal tradition and wish to assimilate into the ethnic melting pot of the Philippines. The past experience and the present plight of the mountain tribespeople demonstrates that the oldest traditions are the most vulnerable to cultural contamination. The mountain tribes have survived foreign invasion, occupation, epidemics and forced labor but corruption by modern technology and materialism may yet prove to be their ultimate downfall. These tribes bear the burden of a troubled history, but they always seem to survive with remarkable grace and equanimity, although many of the elders communicate a palpable sense of despair concerning the future fate of their people. With modern industrial civilization slowly overtaking the villages and many neighboring tribes already extinct, a conscious effort to preserve the ancient rituals, social structures, and religious beliefs will have to be made if the Bontoc, Ifugao, and Kalinga way of life is to endure.

100 year old Kalinga female in the village of Luplupa 1993

Ifugao females in the village of Tam-an 1995

Ifugao tribe in Banaue 1994

Ifugao females in Banaue 1994

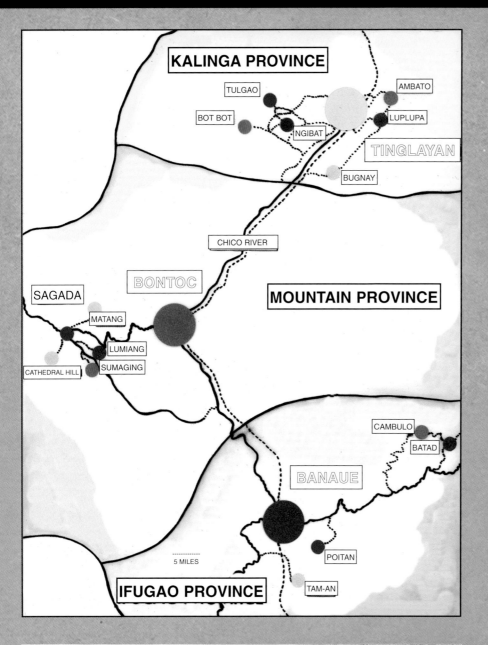

KALINGA PROVINCE

TULGAO

AMBATO

BOT BOT

LUPLUPA

NGIBAT

TINGLAYAN

BUGNAY

CHICO RIVER

BONTOC

MOUNTAIN PROVINCE

SAGADA

MATANG

LUMIANG

SUMAGING

CATHEDRAL HILL

CAMBULO

BATAD

BANAUE

POITAN

5 MILES

IFUGAO PROVINCE

TAM-AN

The Bontoc, Kalinga and Ifugao tribes have approximately two hundred villages each, with populations ranging from fifty to one hundred or more inhabitants in a typical village. The photographs, artifacts and lexicon translations collected and presented within this book were procured from just twelve of the villages: Ambato, Luplupa, Bugnay, Bot-Bot, Ngibat, Tulgao, Poblacion, Batad, Cambulo, Poitan, Tam-an, and Sagada, all found in outlying areas around the small towns of Bontoc, Banaue, and Tinglayan, along the Chico River. Additional artifacts were culled from institutions and private collections in the hope of establishing a valid aesthetic criteria.

The Chico River and its many tributaries are the main source of drinking, bathing and irrigation water for the tribes. The extensive irrigated rice terraces of the region are aptly described by the "locals" as the "eighth wonder of the world." Rice paddy farming has been the basic method of subsistence agriculture in the region since ancient times, and the elegant terraced construction of the paddies is a proud result of thousands of years of continuous cultivation and maintenance.

The mountain tribes inhabit small villages which are primitive by almost any standard, lacking in the most basic amenities: running water, electricity, sewage disposal and modern communication links to the outside world. Living in huts made only of wood and straw, the people prepare their simple subsistence diet, mainly rice and beans with occasional meat dishes, over open hearth fires.

BELIEF

Ifugao tribesman (above)

Rice terrace detail (below)

The village of Batad surrounded by rice terraces (facing page)

(The maps' boxed areas contain the villages visited to collect the tribal beliefs and artifacts in this book)

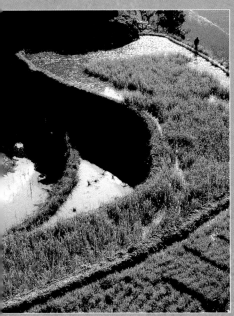

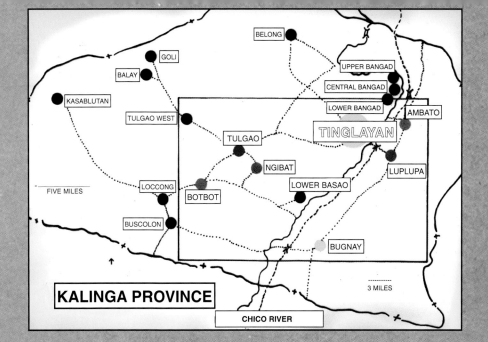

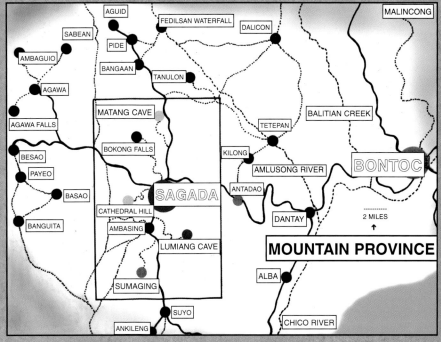

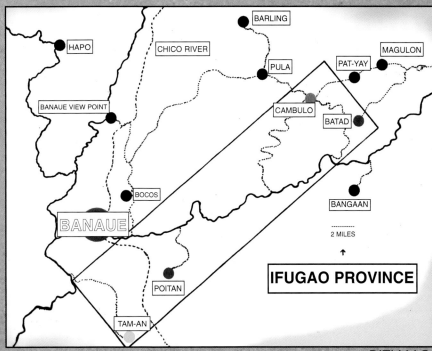

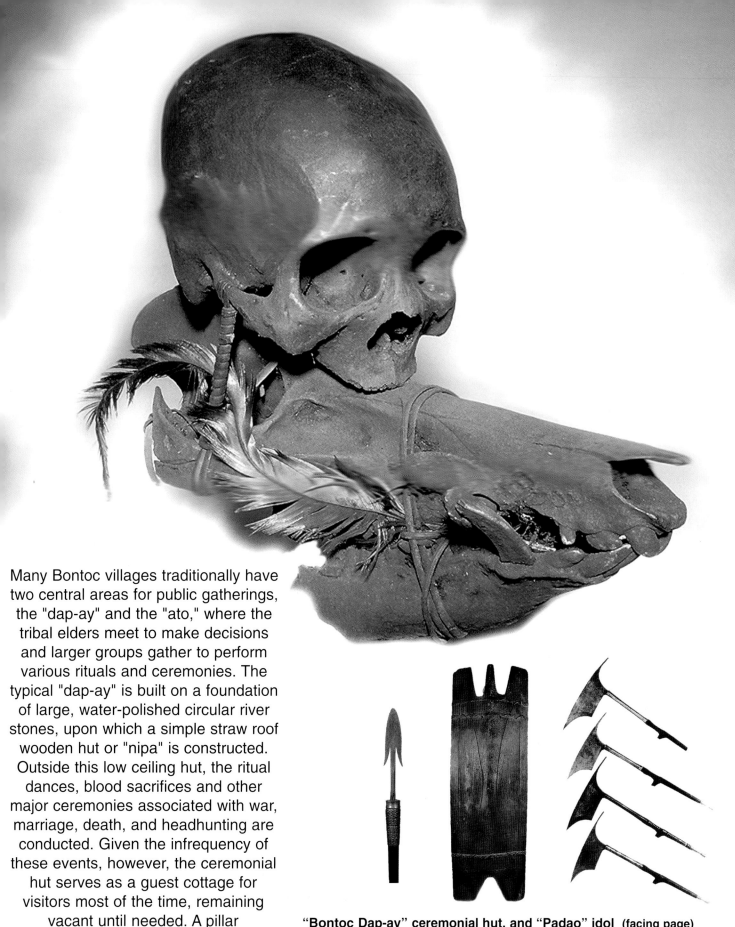

Many Bontoc villages traditionally have two central areas for public gatherings, the "dap-ay" and the "ato," where the tribal elders meet to make decisions and larger groups gather to perform various rituals and ceremonies. The typical "dap-ay" is built on a foundation of large, water-polished circular river stones, upon which a simple straw roof wooden hut or "nipa" is constructed. Outside this low ceiling hut, the ritual dances, blood sacrifices and other major ceremonies associated with war, marriage, death, and headhunting are conducted. Given the infrequency of these events, however, the ceremonial hut serves as a guest cottage for visitors most of the time, remaining vacant until needed. A pillar wooden idol known as a "padao" is sometimes placed in front of or near the ceremonial huts, serving as a protective deity for the tribe.

"Bontoc Dap-ay" ceremonial hut, and "Padao" idol (facing page)
"Ifugao" boar and human skull headhunting trophy (top)
"Kalinga" headhunting spear, shield, and "pinagas" axes (above)
(Axes: Field Museum # 18590)

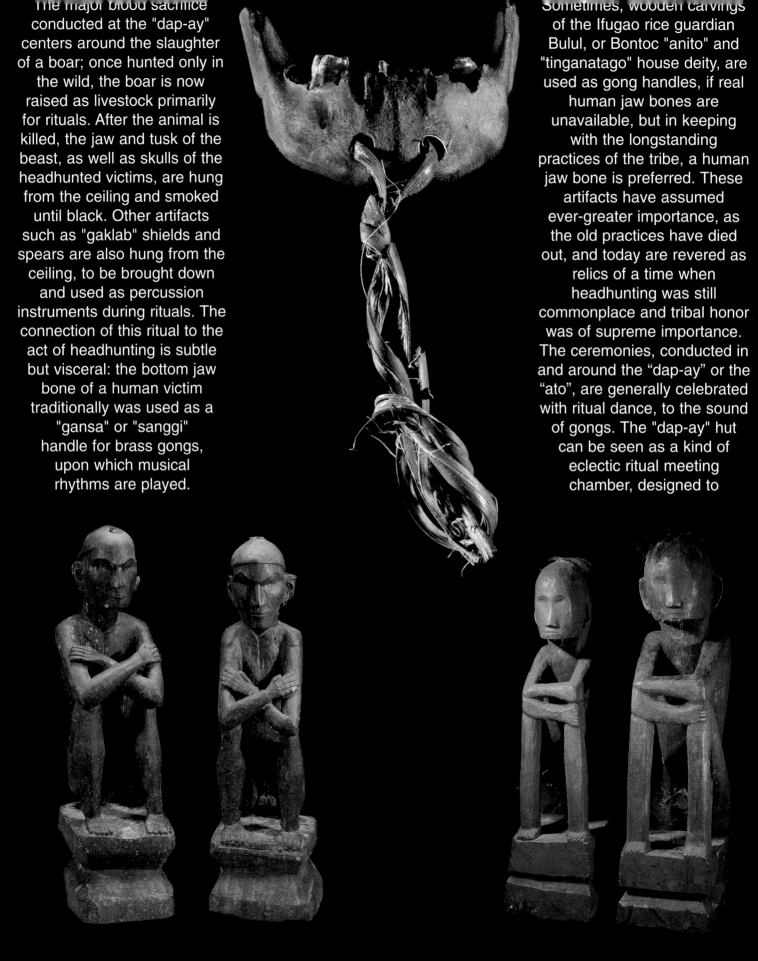

The major blood sacrifice conducted at the "dap-ay" centers around the slaughter of a boar; once hunted only in the wild, the boar is now raised as livestock primarily for rituals. After the animal is killed, the jaw and tusk of the beast, as well as skulls of the headhunted victims, are hung from the ceiling and smoked until black. Other artifacts such as "gaklab" shields and spears are also hung from the ceiling, to be brought down and used as percussion instruments during rituals. The connection of this ritual to the act of headhunting is subtle but visceral: the bottom jaw bone of a human victim traditionally was used as a "gansa" or "sanggi" handle for brass gongs, upon which musical rhythms are played.

Sometimes, wooden carvings of the Ifugao rice guardian Bulul, or Bontoc "anito" and "tinganatago" house deity, are used as gong handles, if real human jaw bones are unavailable, but in keeping with the longstanding practices of the tribe, a human jaw bone is preferred. These artifacts have assumed ever-greater importance, as the old practices have died out, and today are revered as relics of a time when headhunting was still commonplace and tribal honor was of supreme importance. The ceremonies, conducted in and around the "dap-ay" or the "ato", are generally celebrated with ritual dance, to the sound of gongs. The "dap-ay" hut can be seen as a kind of eclectic ritual meeting chamber, designed to

accommodate all the emotional, physical, and metaphysical needs of the tribe. The "ato," in contrast, serves more as a public political forum and meeting place for the tribal elders, who congregate daily to debate tribal affairs and make important decisions. The "ato" is an uncovered court with large stones for seats, so meetings are conducted only as weather permits, but discussion and presentation of individual viewpoints occurs on a regular basis. Like the "dap-ay," the "ato" is rarely visited by female members of the tribe, but the women do actively participate in the support system of the tribe as a whole.

"Sanggi": gong handle, made from a headhunting victims lower jaw, collected in the Kalinga village of Ambato
(facing page, top)

Ifugao "bulul" idol pairs
(facing page, bottom left: Fowler Museum of Cultural History LX 80.367 & .368)

Ifugao male and female ritual dancers
(top right and left: The Field Museum # 32326)

Ifugao "bulul" idol
(The Metropolitan Museum of Art # 1992.24: this page center)

The eating habits of the tribes are intricately woven into the fabric of rituals and daily life. The leaders and elders are given the pick of the sacrificial meats, eating them in isolation, after which the other members of the tribe may consume the leftovers. Special figurine wooden ladles and spoons are used on holidays, to serve portions of sacrificial meat on the "dalolos"; a large circular wooden plate.

Clockwise from the top:
Boar's jawbone and coconut ladle:
(collected in the Ifugao village of Batad)
Ifugao food bowl:
(Peabody Museum, Harvard # 8-36-70/74013)
Ifugao spoon:
(Metropolitan Museum of Art # 1988.143.137)
Ifugao ladle: (Newark Museum # 47.374)
Ifugao ladle: (Newark Museum # 47.376)
Ifugao spoon: (Newark Museum # 47.354)

Traditionally, exceptional wooden spoons, with carved "bulul" figure designs, are frequently used by guests at feasts, if the host is affluent, but usually the tribe eats with their hands, or a small supply of spoons maybe shared. Over the years these carved wooden implements are blackened by smoke from open air hearths, just as the boar's jawbone handle from the ceremonial coconut shell ladle becomes blackened with age. Hot liquids, meats and vegetables are distributed from large pots to smaller containers for personal consumption. Great importance is placed on saving and storing surplus food for use in lean times.

Kalinga "topil" basket:
(collected in the village of Tulgao)
left

Kalinga "agawen" basket:
(collected in the village of Tulgao)
right

Ifugao brooms:
(collected on the island of Mindanao)

Kalinga "benale" basket:
(collected in the village of Tulgao)
middle

Kalinga "agawen" baskets:
(collected in the village of Tulgao)
below

Food is stored in a variety of large baskets.
Smaller baskets serve to carry daily individual
portions. A cleverly designed "agawen" basket is
carried on the hip by toiling rice workers; as they
harvest, plant or tend to the paddies, while looking
for and gathering snails for later consumption.
Brooms, also made from rattan, are used to sweep
out the huts and adjacent stone surfaces.

Handwoven baskets are worn as backpacks to carry food back and forth to work in the fields, on hunting trips, and on visits to neighboring villages. A small, square-shaped lunchbox called a "topil" is tied with string or fiber to hold the top in place. Utility vessels, made of woven rattan, carry necessities on outings, day trips or work sessions. Long term storage of rice, in private huts, is done in a unique conically-shaped "benale" basket.

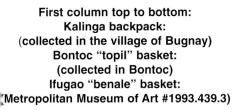

First column top to bottom:
Kalinga backpack:
(collected in the village of Bugnay)
Bontoc "topil" basket:
(collected in Bontoc)
Ifugao "benale" basket:
(Metropolitan Museum of Art #1993.439.3)

second column top to bottom:
Bontoc "topil" basket:
(collected in Bontoc)
Bontoc "benale" basket:
(Eduardo Masferre collection)

Bontoc "benale" basket:
(Eduardo Masferre collection)
Bontoc "agawen" basket:
(Natural History Museum of Los Angeles # a.5011.41-51)

third column top to bottom:
Bontoc basket: (Metropolitan Museum of Art # 1988.143.31)
Bontoc "agawen" basket:
(Eduardo Masferre collection)
Bontoc "topil" basket: (Fowler Museum, U.C.L.A. # LX 78-645 A,B)

This multipurpose use of basketry extends to circular Bontoc hats, known as "socyop" or "balacka," which are also used to carry food and valuables. Kalinga males also wear "o-kong" hats made of more elaborate woven materials, adorned with beautifully colored beads and, in some cases, two mother-of-pearl double circles on either side of the tiny hat, which is held on the head with a string of beads. Of the three tribal cultures, the Kalinga have the reputation of being the most aggressive and physically demonstrative, but all three groups have very similar systems of visual and verbal communication which manifest individual status, experience and authority. The most graphic forms of physical adornment are body tattoos which vividly express the prowess of the bearer. The few surviving Kalinga headhunters, for example, display a large "fatoc" tattoo on their chests. This is usually an abstract geometric blue pattern extending from the top of the abdomen up to the neck and occasionally over the shoulders. Such a martial tattoo can be compared to the medals and patches worn by officers in the modern

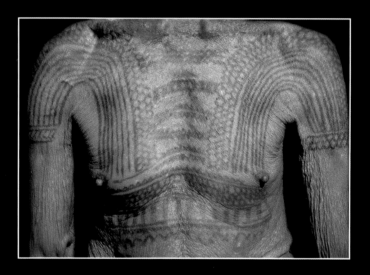

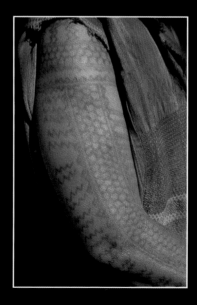

military, indicating the holder's rank, acts of heroism, and performance in the field. Bontoc warriors ware similar "chak-lang" tattoos, as do the Ifugao but chest tattoos are infrequently displayed among these tribes, indicating the custom is no longer practiced, even among the oldest males. The "fatoc" tattoos of the Kalinga females can still be seen today, as can the female Bontoc's "pango" tattoos. Women's tattoos have a different placement and meaning than those of the men, serving primarily to enhance physical appearance rather than to advertise conquests. The Bontoc and Kalinga women sometimes tattoo their entire arms, from the wrist to the shoulders, with equally intricate designs in a deep indigo or blue-colored pattern; smaller tattoos on the face, back, and neck may be worn accenting the total visual effect. The Bontoc and Kalinga women's tattoos show both physical maturity and beauty, just as a western woman might advertise her adulthood by wearing makeup and jewelry.

Kalinga "o-kong" hat:
(collected in the village of Bugnay)
top
Kalinga "fatoc" headhunters tattoo:
center
Kalinga female "fatoc" tattoo:
bottom

Bontoc, Ifugao, and Kalinga males
"socyop", "balacka", and "o-kong" hats
The feather and skull adorned are
ceremonial headdresses. The others are for
hunting or everyday use. Collected in the
villages of BotBot, Batad, and Sagada

The males and females of all three tribal groups use abstract geometric designs which are distinctive and recognizable from a distance as a visual display of tribal affiliation and physical beauty. Although both men and women have traditionally clothed only the bottom half of their bodies, this dress is full of rich symbolic and graphic detail. A short loin cloth, the Kalinga male's "fa-ar", is as fully covered with geometric designs as his female Kalinga counterpart's "ai-in" skirt. The Ifugao male's "binohilen" loincloth and the Ifugao female's "tapis" also indicate tribal membership with a specific design or pattern, as do the clothing designs of the Bontoc tribe.

Among the Kalinga and Bontoc females, additional abstract geometric designs are worn along with the "tapis," in the form of a thick woven textile fringed belt or "tacyard," which hangs down the woman' back.

Facing page first column top to bottom:
Ifugao "tapis" females skirt
Kalinga "ai-in" females skirt
Four Bontoc made, Kalinga worn, "tacyard" females fringed belts

Facing page top to bottom second column:
Kalinga "fa-ar" males loin cloth
Ifugao shamans ritual robe
Bontoc "tacyard" females belt

This page top left: Kalinga "fa-ar" males loin cloth
top right: Bontoc "tapis" females skirt
insets above: Bontoc female wearing a "tacyard" fringed belt
Ifugao woman weaving: (The Field Museum # A 22291)
Kalinga "fa-ar" males loin cloth

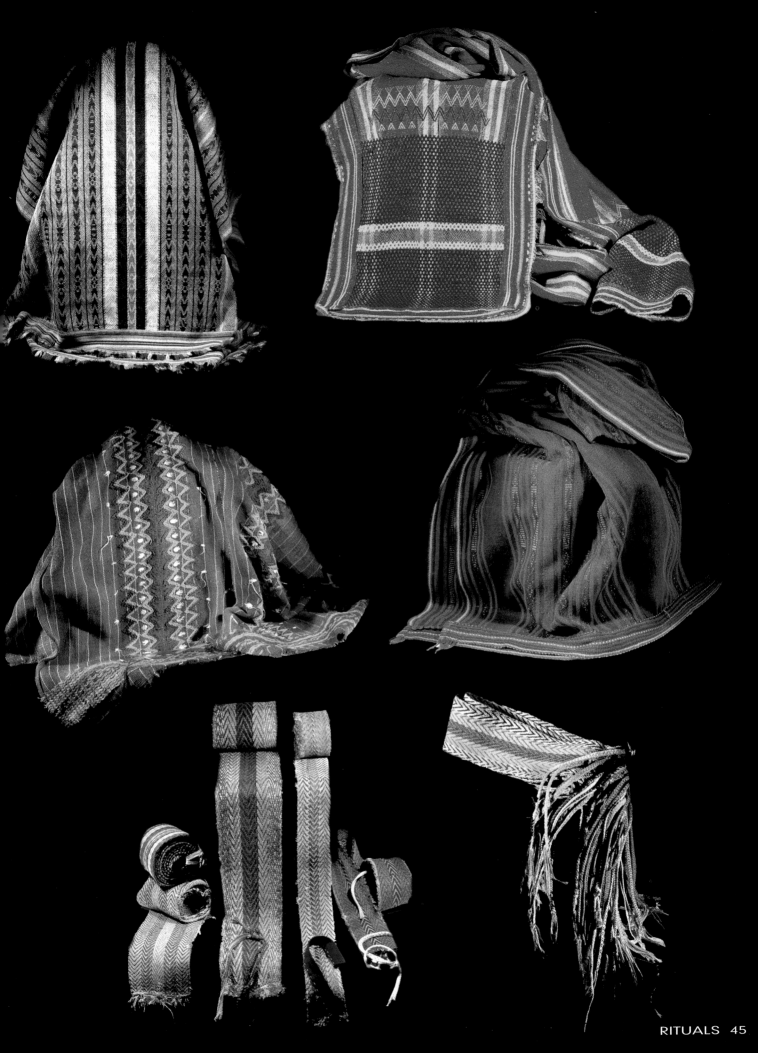

Ifugao males carry a kind of purse, known as a "butung," with a distinct tribal pattern, which is held by a circular coiled brass handle. The handle is highly-prized by the owner, and the possessor of a particularly ornate bag will be the envy of his neighbors. Bontoc women use snake vertebrae, interwoven with colorful beads, to form a magic amulet, worn in the hair like a halo to protect them from thunder and lightning and seen as inducing fertility. These visual elements create a striking, harmonious aesthetic whole when the body tattoos, garments and accoutrements are simultaneously exhibited by an entire tribe. The females of the tribe characteristically pay greater attention to bodily adornment than do the males. Women wear heavy metal earrings, called a "linglingo," the oval shape of which is intended to suggest fertility. These earrings are so heavy they sometimes stretch the ear lobes down to the shoulders; this is considered to be a hallmark of beauty, and a sign of female fertility heralding success in procreation. Similar fertility charms are also worn by men and women as neck pendants, such as the Bontoc "pinangpanga" or the Kalinga "lufay," which are believed to enhance reproductive power. "Fongor," multi-strand beaded necklaces, are worn by Kalinga females, adding to the abstract visual effect of their ornate tattoos and multiple-design zig-zag pattern dresses.

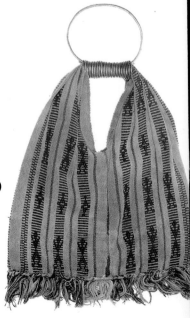

Facing page: three Bontoc "linglingo" fertility charms
(The Natural History Museum of Los Angeles # A.5011.41-10)
two Ifugao silver "linglingo" winged earrings:
(The Brooklyn Museum # 81.45.4&5)

A silver Bontoc "pinangpanga" pendant: (top right)
and four Kalinga "lufay" fertility charms: (bottom)
this page: Ifugao status symbol "butung" bags
(The Newark Museum # 30.571): (left)
Bontoc snake vertebrae amulet: (middle)

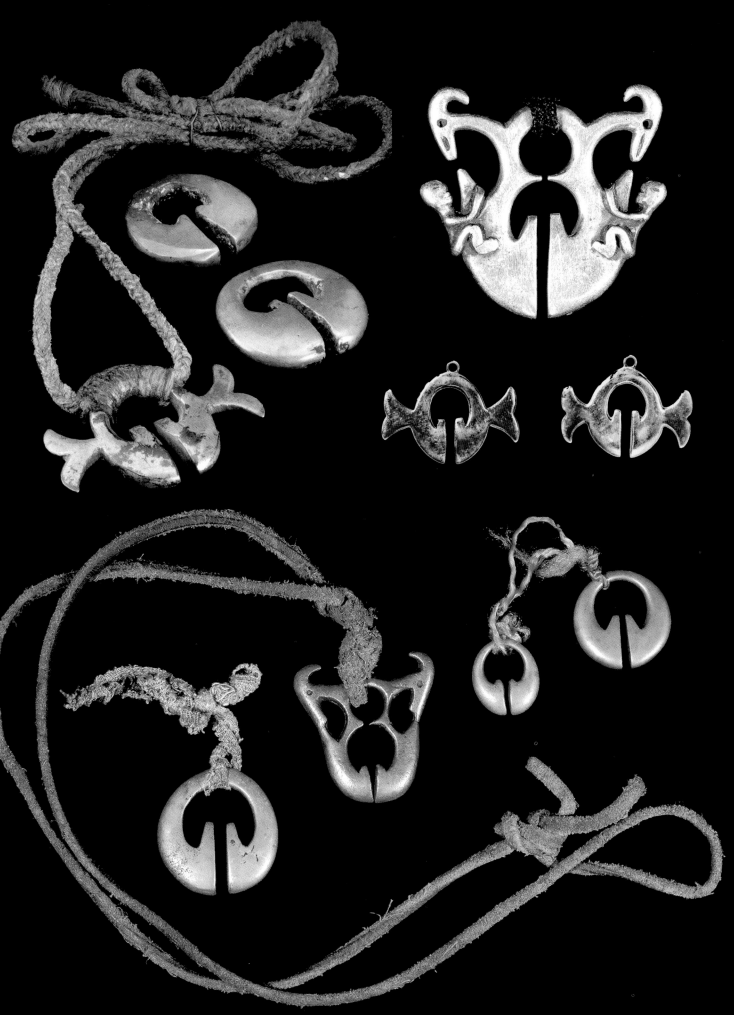

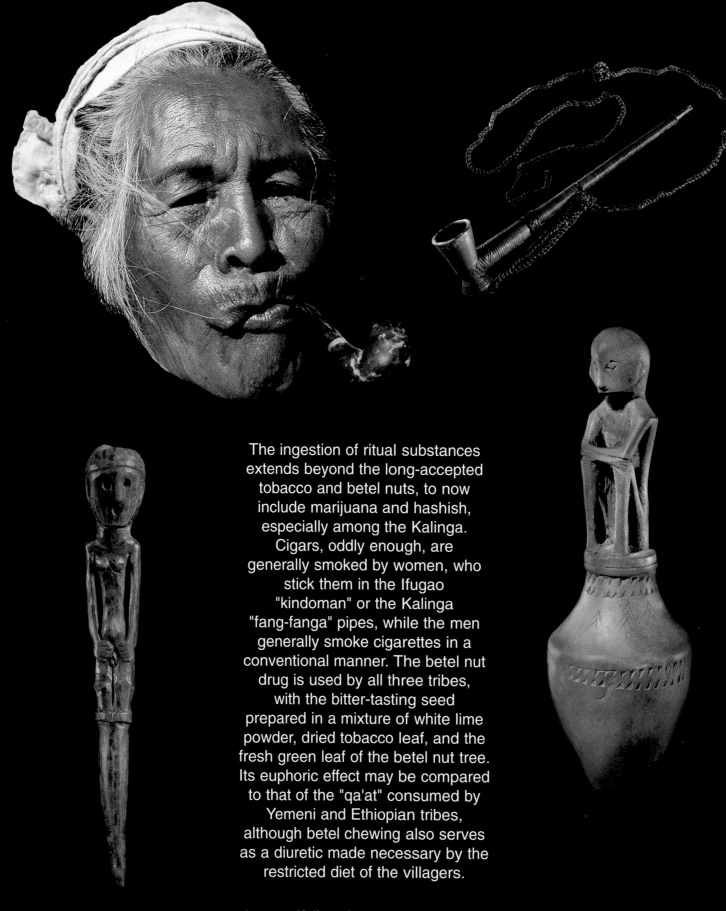

The ingestion of ritual substances extends beyond the long-accepted tobacco and betel nuts, to now include marijuana and hashish, especially among the Kalinga. Cigars, oddly enough, are generally smoked by women, who stick them in the Ifugao "kindoman" or the Kalinga "fang-fanga" pipes, while the men generally smoke cigarettes in a conventional manner. The betel nut drug is used by all three tribes, with the bitter-tasting seed prepared in a mixture of white lime powder, dried tobacco leaf, and the fresh green leaf of the betel nut tree. Its euphoric effect may be compared to that of the "qa'at" consumed by Yemeni and Ethiopian tribes, although betel chewing also serves as a diuretic made necessary by the restricted diet of the villagers.

(above): **Kalinga female smoking a pipe**

(bottom left): **Ifugao betel nut crusher**

(bottom right): **Ifugao betel nut lime container** (University of Pennsylvania Museum of Anthropology # P-2101)

(top right): **Bontoc pipe** (Natural History Museum of Los Angeles # A.2043.29-7)

The most important rituals of the tribes center around birth, puberty, marriage, death, the rice harvest, rice wine fermentation and up until recently, headhunting! For all three tribes, the rice harvest ritual is the most important, conceptually combining the tribe's philosophy, religion, and art with their basic means

of survival. Among the Ifugao, "bulul" rice guardian figures are stored in the rice granary as familiar protective spirits and traditionally taken out only at harvest time. As many as four to eight pair of these figures may inhabit granaries filled with the bounty from the enormous rice terraces in the hills beyond.

(above center): Ifugao ceremonial "bulul" with bracelets, indicating an affluent owner.

(left): Ifugao "bulul" from the village of Poitan

(right): Ifugao "bulul" from the village of Lagaue

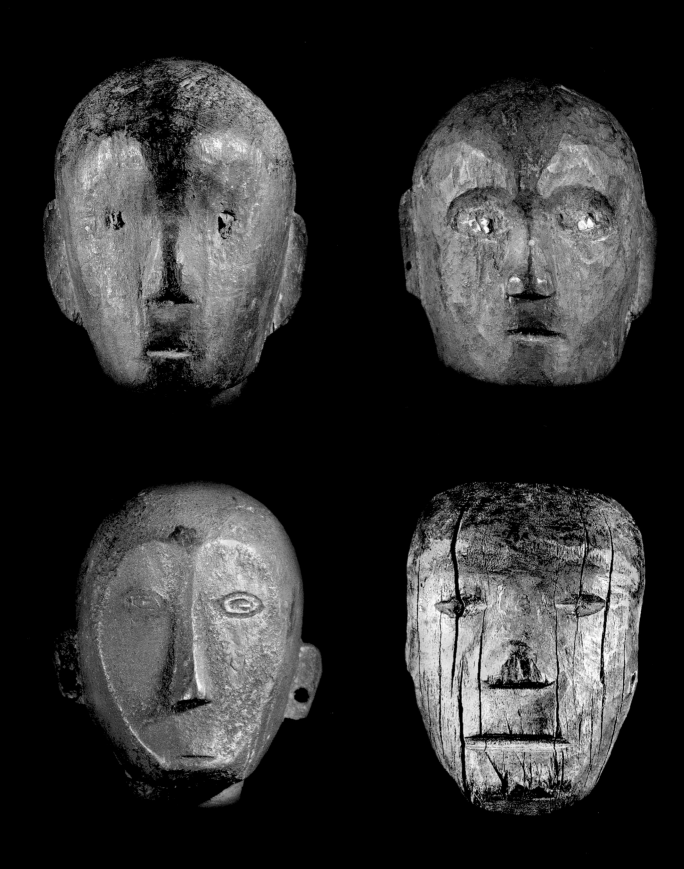

(top and bottom left): **Three Ifugao "bulul"** (facial details)

(bottom right): **Bontoc "anito"** (facial detail)

(top left): Bontoc "padao (facial detail)

(top right and bottom): Three Ifugao "bulul" (facial details)

In addition to the seated "bulul", the tribes also
carve singular standing "bululs" and "ancestor" pairs.

(facing page center): **Ifugao standing "ancestor bulul" pair**
(left): **Ifugao seated and standing "bulul" pair**
(right): **Ifugao standing "bulul" pair**

(this page center): **Ifugao rice wine ritual standing "bulul"**
(left): **Two pairs of standing Ifugao "ancestor bulul"**
(top right): **Ifugao standing "bulul"**
(bottom right): **Ifugao "dancing bulul"**

The "punam-han" is a ritual offertory box used by the Ifugao in conjunction with the "bulul" idols. A "hipag" or carved wooden idol similar in form to the "bulul" but representing a more warlike spirit is sometimes placed in the "punam-han" sacrificial wooden box along with betel nuts, rice, meat, and optional bound fetishes consisting of sticks, feathers, beaks, feet or other animal parts, as an offering to the Ifugao gods.

(top left): Ifugao "punam-han" ceremonial box in the form of a man holding a box
(The Fowler Museum U.C.L.A. # LX 80-268)
(bottom left): Ifugao "punam-han" as the human form holding a box, Cambulo village
(right top): Ifugao "hipag" (The Hearst Museum of Anthropology # 10-2807)
(right middle): Ifugao "hipag", Tam-an village
(bottom right): Ifugao "bulul" pair on top of a "punam-han" sacrificial box

Five Ifugao "punam-han" ritual offertory boxes

(center)
The Fowler Museum of Cultural History
U.C.L.A. # LX 78-951 A,B

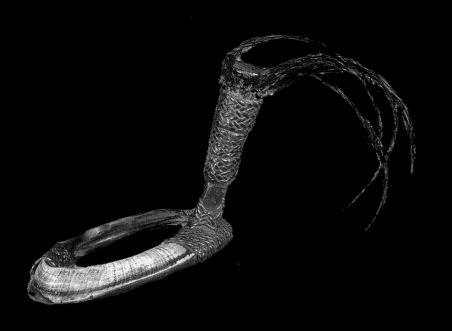

In Kalinga tradition, the hair of a head hunting victim may be dyed red and attached to boar tusks, forming a kind of bracelet called the "tuckar" which is passed down through generations and worn by the men during rituals and other important ceremonies.

(this page left):
Three Bontoc ritual boar tusk bracelets
(The Natural History Museum of Los Angeles #A2043.29-4)

(top): Two Kalinga "tuckar" boar tusk bracelets with the hair of a head hunted human victim

(facing page):
Two Kalinga "tuckar" boar tusk bracelets with the hair of a head hunted victim, beads and feathers

Bontoc and Ifugao males wear boar tusk bracelets also, but instead of human hair, a small wooden carving of a "bulul" rice guardian or other human form is attached, resembling the figures found on their gong handles. The Bontoc refer to this bracelet as a "tongkil." All three tribes may wear the wristlet higher up as an armband, if the boar tusks happen to be large enough.

Ritual headhunting has been illegal in the Philippines for almost one hundred years, but there have been reports of incidents as recently as the 1970s. Some of the tribes are closer to the old ways than others. For example, the Kalinga headhunters' "falos" ritual may still be performed whenever the formal "bopong" peace pact is violated, or after a serious personal slight. A vendetta is declared and revenge becomes a matter of tribal and individual honor. A typical dispute might involve rape, murder or theft caused by a visitor or rival from another tribe.

In the past, of course, nothing less than full retribution would suffice.

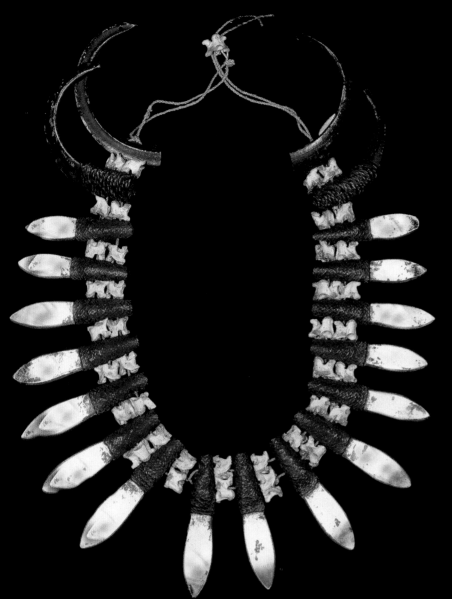

(facing page top left):
Kalinga ritual head hunting ceremonial beads and boar tusk necklace
(top right): **Ifugao shell and fiber necklace**
(bottom left): **Bontoc "boaya" head hunters bone and boar tusk necklace**
(bottom right): **Bontoc female shell and bone dowry belt**

(this page top):
Bontoc "boaya" carved shell, bone, and boar tusk ritual head hunting necklace
(bottom): **Ifugao shell and fiber necklace**
(The Metropolitan Museum of Art #1993.439.2)

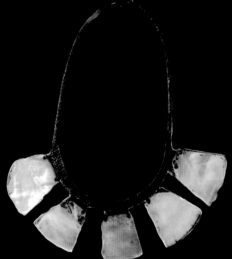

Once the vendetta was declared, the selection of an exchange victim was fairly arbitrary; any member of the opposing tribe would suffice to settle the blood price. There was rarely anything personal about the choice of a victim, particularly during the heat of battle, when members of rival clans or villages were struggling for the sacred honor of the tribe. Before a headhunting expedition, male warriors gathered at the "dap-ay" wearing all of the traditional ceremonial ornaments, including bone or shell "boaya" or "pangapang" necklaces, ornate head dresses and boar tusk armbands. While performing rituals, the fully adorned warriors prepared themselves emotionally and physically for the hunt.

A headless Ifugao being carried away for burial on his own shield Banana, Nueva Wizcaya. Philippine Isl. about 1904? Col L M Maus Photo

(this page top row left): Kalinga spear (center): **Ifugao headhunting victim being carried away on his own shield 1904** (the Smithsonian Institution #56702) (right): **Ifugao warrior** (The Field Museum #A 22083) (bottom row left): **Headhunting ax head** (The Natural History Museum of Los Angeles # A.601450-4) (center): **Lime pouch, tobacco case, and knife** (left): **"bolo" machete** (facing page top row left): **Ifugao headhunter with victims skull** (The American Museum of Natural History #2128) (center): **Ifugao headhunter warrior with victims skulls** (The Field Museum #22231) (right): **Ifugao headhunting trophies and sacrificed animal skulls** (The American Museum of Natural History #2131) (bottom row left): **Kalinga ""pinagas" headhunting ax** (bottom right): **Four Bontoc "kalasag" shields** (The Field Museum #18571)

In the Bontoc headhunting dance and ritual called "bangi-bang," the "gaklab" miniature shields are brought out, exhibited and then tapped rhythmically. A ritual dance can continue for hours, until each warrior falls into a trance-like state and takes up his weapons. The older Kalinga men still perform the preparatory "lalo" headhunting dance, waving their "tobi" spears and "pinagas" axes, even if their "foronit" headhunting days are past. A lead rhythm is sounded, initiating the "falos" ritual, and the dancers answer with a counter rhythm on their hand-held gongs, building into a pattern of call and response. The group moves single file in a circle and, upon a designated beat, reverses and dances in the opposite direction.

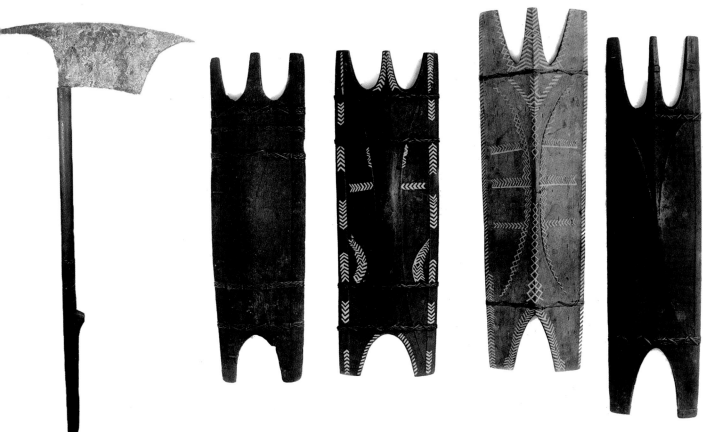

The three essential implements for headhunting are the spear, the shield and the ax. Each tribe has special names for these ritual weapons. The Bontoc refer to the full-size shield as the "kalasag," the spear as the "tufay," and the headhunting ax as the "kaman." Regardless of the name, the deadly effects are the same. The long spear serves to wound and bring down the opponent in battle. The shield's curved bottom is then used to pin down the struggling victim by the neck. The heavy flat blade of the double-sided ax performs the actual decapitation, and the sharply curved opposing side is used to skin the skull. A more purposeful and workmanlike approach to this grisly task cannot be imagined.

(top left): Headhunted victims jaw bone used as a handle on the musical gongs played in rituals
(middle left): Headhunting trophy skull
(top right): Headhunting skull with rattan strap
(middle right): Headhunting jaw bone gong handle
(bottom row): Four headhunting trophies
(facing page top right): Four headhunting skulls held within a carabao jaw mounted on a post
(top left): Headhunting trophy wrapped in snake skin
(bottom center): Headhunted human skull mounted on a pigs skull
(bottom left and right): Headhunted victim jaw bone gong handles

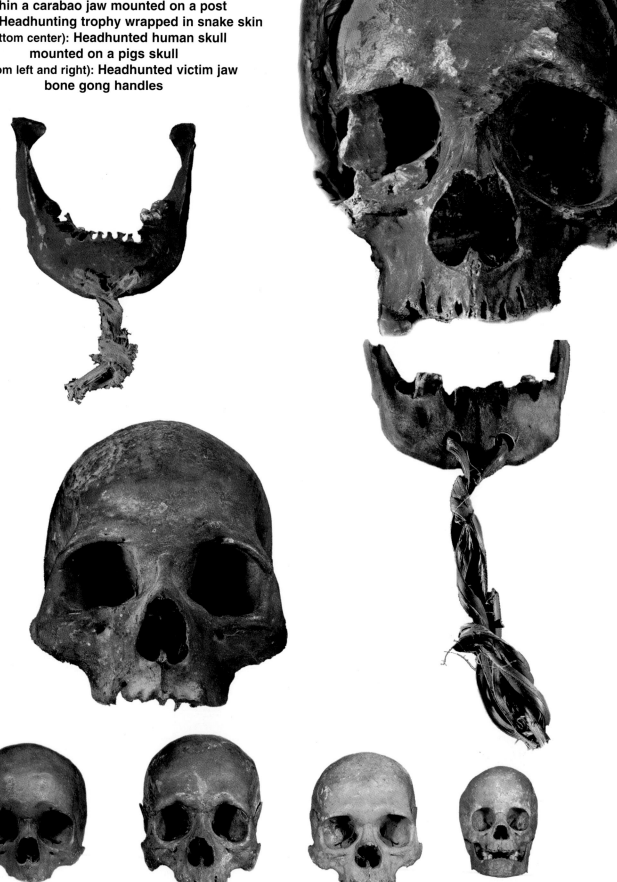

A superficial interpretation of headhunting might lead Western observers to conclude that these are simply pagan savages engaging in a barbarous and meaningless custom. Closer examination, however, reveals the headhunting rituals to be highly-structured religious ceremonies involving spiritual and emotional empowerment. These rituals serve to resolve intertribal disputes and to balance the scales of justice. To condemn the practice as barbarous is to misunderstand an important and necessary means of restoring social order and normalizing tribal relations, giving the practitioners contact with, and control over, the long cycles of life and death that pervade their primitive cosmos.

TRAVELLING

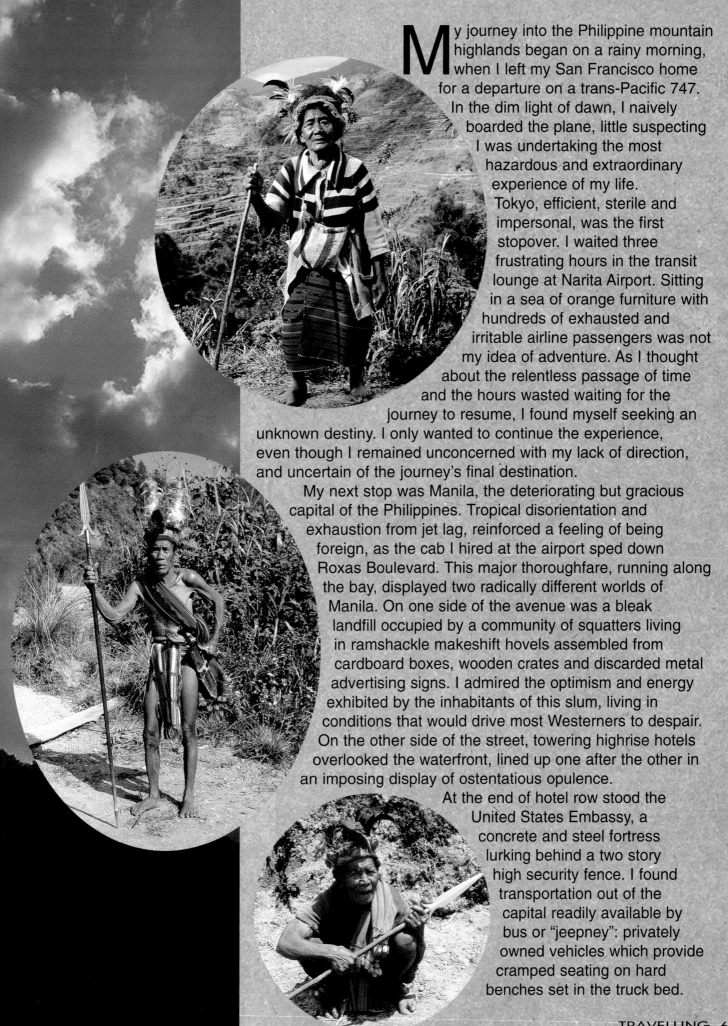

My journey into the Philippine mountain highlands began on a rainy morning, when I left my San Francisco home for a departure on a trans-Pacific 747. In the dim light of dawn, I naively boarded the plane, little suspecting I was undertaking the most hazardous and extraordinary experience of my life.

Tokyo, efficient, sterile and impersonal, was the first stopover. I waited three frustrating hours in the transit lounge at Narita Airport. Sitting in a sea of orange furniture with hundreds of exhausted and irritable airline passengers was not my idea of adventure. As I thought about the relentless passage of time and the hours wasted waiting for the journey to resume, I found myself seeking an unknown destiny. I only wanted to continue the experience, even though I remained unconcerned with my lack of direction, and uncertain of the journey's final destination.

My next stop was Manila, the deteriorating but gracious capital of the Philippines. Tropical disorientation and exhaustion from jet lag, reinforced a feeling of being foreign, as the cab I hired at the airport sped down Roxas Boulevard. This major thoroughfare, running along the bay, displayed two radically different worlds of Manila. On one side of the avenue was a bleak landfill occupied by a community of squatters living in ramshackle makeshift hovels assembled from cardboard boxes, wooden crates and discarded metal advertising signs. I admired the optimism and energy exhibited by the inhabitants of this slum, living in conditions that would drive most Westerners to despair. On the other side of the street, towering highrise hotels overlooked the waterfront, lined up one after the other in an imposing display of ostentatious opulence.

At the end of hotel row stood the United States Embassy, a concrete and steel fortress lurking behind a two story high security fence. I found transportation out of the capital readily available by bus or "jeepney": privately owned vehicles which provide cramped seating on hard benches set in the truck bed.

Everywhere in the Philippines, these gaudily decorated public conveyances wait for paying passengers, departing only when the driver has enough fares to justify the cost of the trip. Filipino buses are only a little more reliable, but much more comfortable, since they are more likely to have seating space and keep to a regular timetable.

The only two ways to get to Bontoc and the surrounding villages of the highlands are by heading north from Manila via Baguio, or through Banaue, one of the larger towns of the Ifugao province. Baguio, a lovely provincial capital with elegant colonial architecture and a relaxed atmosphere, came as a refreshing change of pace after the stress of Manila. From Baguio, I caught an overland bus for the bumpy eight hour ride across the crest of the Cordillera mountain range. The vehicle was a reconditioned school bus with its original child size seats reupholstered, and repainted in the company colors.

We stopped occasionally for the passengers to rest and relieve themselves. The sights and smells on the winding road to Bontoc were bewildering - open air markets with animal carcasses butchered on blood soaked wooden tables; heaps of unidentifiable green gelatinous material in enormous plastic bags; the occasional stench of burning rubber or cloth; garish religious paraphernalia; cold drinks in recycled oil cans, and anxious vendors jumping on and off the bus, pleading and offering questionable food and drink— everything from cooked chicken fetus, in its shell, to cheap gin in small soda bottles. In the distance, rustic huts sent forth faint plumes of smoke curling upward into the humid equatorial atmosphere. The landscape and the settlements became sparse after the first hour of travel, but even at the small town bus stops there were disquieting reminders of the big city urban exiles, like the transvestite waiters at a bizarre village cafe. A paradoxical mixture of old and new reappeared at every roadside stop, as we drove above the clouds crossing countless mountain tops.

Bontoc, the capital of the Mountain Province, is a small town clustered around a street about four blocks long, but it serve as the hub of an extended community of some fifty villages in the vicinity. Transportation by private jeepney can be arranged from Bontoc to various drop off spots for the more remote villages, but past this point foreigners are advised

to travel with a local guide, preferably one from the tribe being visited. My first guide, Juliet, was a short woman of about forty who solicited me as I ate dinner at Bontoc's Mountain Inn, the dollar-a-day hotel where I was lodging. Stout and cheerful, she strolled from table to table striking up conversations with any foreigner, soliciting employment as a guide. With her ebullient air and forceful presentation of self, it seemed she could virtually will travelers to accept her as a confidant and counselor. Eventually she approached me and said in a distinct staccato voice, "Me Juliet. Do you want go rice terraces, burial caves, native village? I be guide! You want go with me?" I was skeptical at first, since Juliet was wearing a handmade native rattan pack that seemed incongruous with her store

bought plaid dress, Nike jacket, and dress shoes unfit for any type of hiking. She agreed to take me to seven of the Kalinga villages, places where the tribespeople still lived in primitive huts and wore traditional native attire. The dirt road from Bontoc to Tinglayan, one of the largest towns in Kalinga province, follows a tortuous route along a steep precipice that falls a half-mile down to the Chico River below. A two hour ride on a commercial bus line had been the only reliable transportation to Tinglayan, but one of the buses hit a Kalinga child who later died. The bus company had to cancel its service through the province to avoid tribal retribution. The only acceptable resolution for the Kalinga would be to take the life of one of the bus drivers, or at the very least some unlucky Bontoc intruder. Eventually, frustrated by the lack of victims, the Kalinga vented their frustration by killing one of their own dogs, so the matter died down of its own accord. This vendetta resulted from breaking the tribal peace pact.

Bontoc

Matang burial caves

The Chico River

Ifugao rice terraces at dawn

Bontoc huts

Kalinga headhunter

Kalinga female

We were the only passengers when we started out from Bontoc, but at every stop more tribes people climbed on board. By the time we arrived the jeepney was packed with elaborately tattooed women, chickens in crates, hundred pound sacks of rice, large rolled tobacco leaves, and clinging children. Walking down the dirt road from the jeepney stop to her friend's hut in Tinglayan, Juliet confessed she was too frightened to go any further than three of the closest villages.

Kalinga headhunter warrior

Juliet explained that her Bontoc tribe was a traditional enemy of the Kalinga, and she would not venture very far into their territory. The Kalinga had recently killed a young Japanese traveller, she warned me, cutting off his ear and penis and leaving him to die in the road as a warning to other intruders. Perhaps he was slain in retribution for the brutal Japanese occupation of the Luzon highlands at the end of the Second World War, where they retreated before their final surrender near Banaue. More likely, he was simply killed for being in the wrong place at the wrong time.

Directly across the Chico river from Tinglayan are the easily accessible Kalinga villages of Ambato and Luplupa, and my guide was willing to take me that far. The remote villages higher up in the mountains, she said, were only to be visited by the most intrepid travellers. The Kalinga are notorious for being the most violent and unpredictable of the mountain people, and although my guide was otherwise capable, I still had to pay tribute to virtually every adult male I met along the trail. The Kalinga are the fiercest warriors within all of the mountain provinces— guerrilla warfare was widespread in the region for decades — and their demands are usually backed up by a small arsenal of spears, machetes, and guns. At Ambato, the first village as we crossed the Chico River, several dozen

elevated huts hovered over a solid pavement of massive stones hauled up from the riverbed. Livestock and poultry wandered freely underneath the cramped one-room huts and between a few ramshackle wood-frame buildings. Half-a-dozen village boys were shooting a homemade basketball into a makeshift hoop made from a vegetable basket nailed to a tree. Against an idyllic natural backdrop of river, jungle and mountains, I was able to photograph my first actual head hunter, a man with the special "fatoc" tattoo on his chest indicating that he had indeed taken heads as a young man. He was a wiry gray-haired old man proudly wearing a bold zig-zaging patterned Kalinga loincloth and holding a long spear in his right hand. He nodded politely as we approached, and smiled broadly when I took his picture, but I never learned anything about him, not even his name because neither Juliet nor I spoke the Kalinga dialect. As we left him, I kept wondering if all the headhunters would be so gentle and accommodating.

As we walked through the village, my guide explained that the government had once tried to dam up the Chico river which would have flooded Ambato and the neighboring villages. The local Kalinga chief rejected the relocation program and was allegedly murdered by government militiamen firing a hail of bullets through the walls of his hut as he slept. The outraged Kalinga continued to fiercely

One of the three 100 year old Kalinga females from Luplupa village

The Kalinga village of Luplupa

esist, and the government finally abandoned its plans. The dam was never completed, reinforcing the Kalinga people's determination to preserve their traditional independence. I followed Juliet a short distance over to the second of the lower villages along the Chico to Luplupa. Larger than Ambato, Luplupa had a small school, a run down church, with huts and houses scattered on several levels. Juliet took me to the oldest women in the village showing me the tattoos that ran from from their shoulders to their wrists. I recognized the same pattern I had seen on the tattooed women loading heavy sacks onto the jeepney we took from Bontoc a short while earlier. Three of the women claimed to be over 100 years old; they allowed me to photograph their heavily-tattooed arms as they squatted in front of their huts.

Juliet and I soon returned to the house of her friend, a single mother with seven boys ranging from three to fourteen years of age. I was exhausted from the day's activities and fell asleep before my host could serve the dinner prepared for us. Juliet, her friend and all seven of the boys later joined me, and we all slept soundly on the floor of the one-room hut The next morning one of the boys named Danee asked if I would

The first Kalinga headhunter encountered from the village of Ambato

The Kalinga village of Ambato

like to take a bath. When I agreed, several of the boys took me down to the river. We spent a happy half-hour bathing in the swift-moving stream, sharing a single bar of soap. Danee asked in broken English, "Is this how Americans take bath?" Several of the boys finished

bathing and ran off into the jungle without a word. I took a leisurely bath and walked alone back to my host's hut, where I discovered one of my cameras had been stolen. The theft of the camera caused me to lose faith in Juliet's role as a goodwill ambassador to the Kalinga, so I asked her to return with me to Bontoc. I wondered what I might lose next— all of my equipment, my freedom, maybe my life. After a grueling two-hour jeepney ride to Bontoc, we finally got back to the "Pines Kitchenette," where I had left my baggage before departing for the Kalinga province.

Juliet was a waitress at the Pines, and upon our return she began serving food and looking for people to guide. I had trusted the innkeepers with all of my baggage and found it secure on my return. When I asked for my luggage however, they accused me of stealing a small photograph that had been hanging in the second floor hallway. The picture in question was a signed print by the well-known Filipino photographer and collector Eduardo Masferre, a vintage hand-tinted work that dated from the 1950's. I was surprised, as well as confused by this allegation, but evidently the dishonor incurred by the camera theft required an equivalent offense on my part. The Bontoc tribal peace pact always calls for retribution — if one head is taken another must be taken in payment. This is the law of the jungle!

The Chico river

The missing hand tinted photograph by
Eduardo Masferre, 1952.
(top left)

Danee asked if I wanted to take a bath in the
Chico river, and the hut we slept in the night
before, 1995. (bottom left)

Boys bathing in the Chico river. One drinks while the other urinates.   (top)

Huts I slept in while travelling among the headhunters. (bottom left and right)

The police were finally convinced of my innocence after a lengthy interview and a thorough search of my belongings. Disillusioned and hungry after hours of interrogation, I returned to the Mountain Inn where I originally met Juliet and booked a room. While ordering a meal, I noticed a hand drawn map of Kalinga villages pinned to the wall of the restaurant. In one corner of the map I saw the notation "Contact Francis Pa-in, Tour Guide." As I ate my chicken adobo, I told my waiter about the problems I had employing a Bontoc guide in Kalinga villages. He told me Francis Pa-in was actually a Kalinga tribesman who could take me anywhere safely since he was well known throughout the Kalinga Province.

The Kalinga necklace acquired in Tinglayan

My waiter disappeared for only a few minutes, and soon Francis Pa-in walked up to me and asked, "Are you looking for me?" I explained my predicament and he seemed to sense my needs. He thought for a moment before he spoke in a gentle tone: "A traveler in our country needs a guide he can trust, or the villagers will never trust him. The person you travel with and the road you travel on are more important than how many villages you see or how many pictures you take."

A Bontoc headhunter warrior holding a box of stick matches, Dean Worcester, American Museum of Natural History, circa 1890, #2071
We traded matches for the right to take photographs

The father burned off the feathers of a chicken

Francis spoke fluent English and had some college education, rare among the mountain people, and I was relieved to hear his fee would be even less than Juliet's. "Don't forget to bring some matches and candy," he added. I was confused by his request, and Francis quickly explained, "The people will let you take their pictures if you give them little gifts." I asked why matches and candy and not something else. Francis replied, "The villagers do not use money, but they have to buy matches. If you give them matches, they don't need any money to survive. They like candy too because it is so hard to get here! So if you give them matches and candy, they are getting a necessity and a luxury! That makes them very happy."

Some time later, as I looked at Dean Worcester's photographs, I noticed a portrait of a head hunter holding a box of stick matches identical to ones I later used to win the confidence and cooperation of the natives. I surmised this modern practice had actually been a local tradition for more than a century.

The following morning I repeated the bumpy two hour jeepney ride back to Tinglayan, this time with Francis my authentic Kalinga guide. The jeepney was so crowded I had to ride on the roof, where my fellow passengers offered me food, drink, and cigarettes. By the time we arrived in Tinglayan, Francis had invited me to spend an unforgettable night with his family.

he family was all traditional Kalinga tribespeople. The ged mother had vivid tattoos all over her face, chest, ck and arms. The geometric patterns on her ess set off the tattoos and stimulated my agination in a way I had never experienced. ancis' elderly father demonstrated the aditional Kalinga method of killing a chicken by ocking its windpipe with a piece of wood until it uffocated. He burned off the feathers over a nall fire and boiled the whole chicken for our vening meal. Francis' uncle had the tattoo signia of a headhunter warrior, so I asked m whether he had any old Kalinga artifacts sell. We quickly agreed on a price for a ass "linglingo" fertility charm, satisfied ith our transaction we both sat down ound a roaring fire.

The mother's Kalinga textile

Vhile we ate and Irank, the other illagers stole into ne shadows and /atched us silently. Vhen Francis' ncle went into the ut and returned vith the necklace, alf a dozen of the nlookers came ut of the dark and resented their wn handicrafts nd goods for sale.

The uncle's brass "linglingo" fertility charm

The accommodations in Tinglayan were spartan, and of course there was no toilet or running water. I was told I could relieve myself right in the front yard, leaving the excre- ment for the pigs to consume. On each side of the house was a grave, placed in the traditional Kalinga tribute to the family ancestors. I was worried about giving offense to the family, but my guide assured me I could urinate out the second story window, to save a trip up and down the stairs. "Don't worry," he went on, "I have done it this way all my life!" I later learned the grave on my side of the house belonged to his sister, who had died of malaria at the age of sixteen while in the neigh- boring Kalinga town of Tabuk. I wondered at their indifference to what should have been a sacred site, but realized the Kalinga concepts of the sacred and profane were too closely related to create any obstacles for a perfectly natural act. Both, life and death, are beautiful within Kalinga, and what seemed unusual at the time I now realize was simply the purest form of innocence!

A Kalinga female jeepney passenger

Riding on top of a jeepney during the second trip, from Bontoc to Tinglayan

**Carabao water buffalo in Kalinga rice terraces (top)
The "endless" stairway,
on the way to Tulgao village (bottom)**

Across from Tinglayan proper is a steep mountain ridge, to cross which required an entire day of climbing, one step at a time, over a seemingly endless stairway running up and over the crest. In the noonday heat, we made our way over the hand-hewn stone steps. Placed to offer a secure footing on the slippery hillside during the rainy season. The stones turned fiery hot in the blazing sun. My feet began to swell and blister, but Francis was as oblivious to the heat as an Indian firewalker strolling across a bed of burning coals. We finally arrived late that afternoon in the mountain village of Tulgao. A great festival was in progress, celebrating the males' adolescent passage into manhood. The Kalinga leaders put me in a place of honor up on a small stage. The stage served as a viewing stand to observe the

**A palm tree reflected in a Kalinga rice terrace (top)
The ritual slaughter of
carabao, cooked in Tulgao village (bottom)**

games, dances, and rituals being performed. A large water buffalo or "carabao" was slaughtered. Large chunks of raw meat were being cut up into five inch cubes and laid out on banana leaves on the bare ground. Blood was spattered everywhere — on the ground, on the cooking pots, and on their clothing. Two large kettles containing the entrails and blood of the animal were boiling rapidly. During ritual feasts, the elite Kalinga males always eat the choicest parts of the ceremonial foods in isolation away from the women and children; this is the Kalinga custom and this feast proved to be no exception. As the men began filing into a windowless wooden structure, one turned and beckoned to Francis. This signal was an invitation for us to dine in seclusion, with Tulgao's Kalinga leaders.

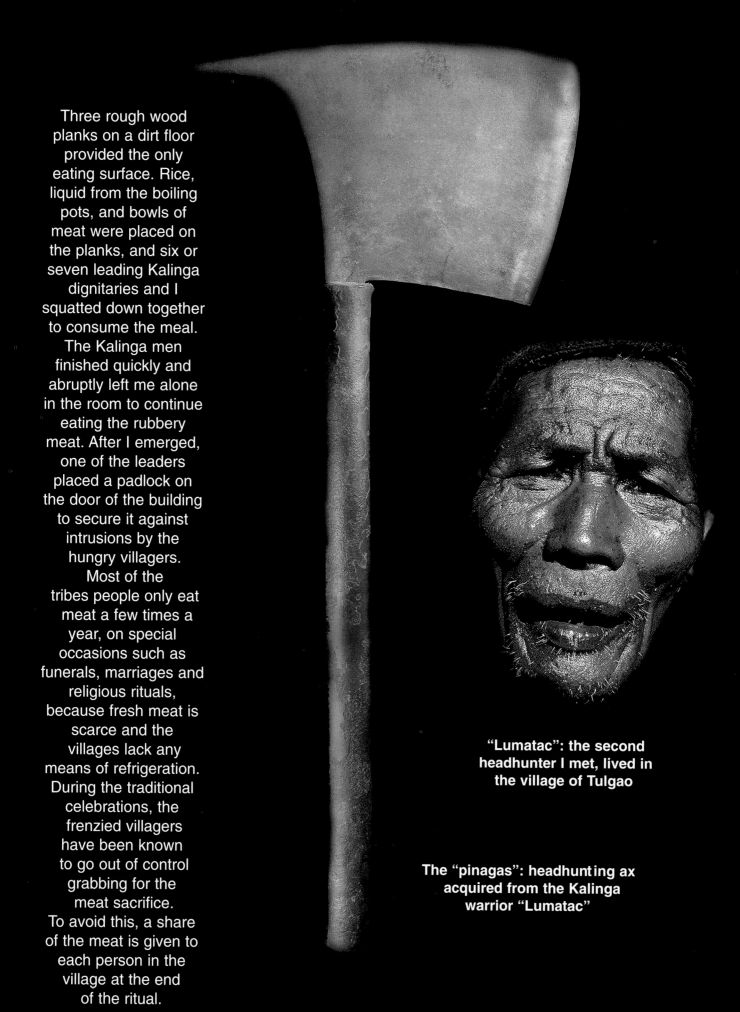

Three rough wood planks on a dirt floor provided the only eating surface. Rice, liquid from the boiling pots, and bowls of meat were placed on the planks, and six or seven leading Kalinga dignitaries and I squatted down together to consume the meal.

The Kalinga men finished quickly and abruptly left me alone in the room to continue eating the rubbery meat. After I emerged, one of the leaders placed a padlock on the door of the building to secure it against intrusions by the hungry villagers.

Most of the tribes people only eat meat a few times a year, on special occasions such as funerals, marriages and religious rituals, because fresh meat is scarce and the villages lack any means of refrigeration. During the traditional celebrations, the frenzied villagers have been known to go out of control grabbing for the meat sacrifice.

To avoid this, a share of the meat is given to each person in the village at the end of the ritual.

"Lumatac": the second headhunter I met, lived in the village of Tulgao

The "pinagas": headhunting ax acquired from the Kalinga warrior "Lumatac"

A thick rattan fiber is threaded through the large chunks, so that the individual tribes people can carry the portions back to their huts. A short while after this heavy meal, as the dancing and music continued, a teenager wearing a peace symbol pendant around his neck sauntered up to me and struck up a conversation. When I said I was an American, he told me a little more about himself. He was sixteen years old, loved American rock and roll, and was a devout Christian. He was as proud of his blue jeans, leather jacket and sneakers as any streetwise American teenager, but to me he seemed a figure trapped in an alien time and place, carrying a foreign message of love and peace in the midst of a primitive headhunting culture. It took him a while to understand that I was more interested in his culture than my own. I was skeptical of his Western attitude and dress, but when I told him I was looking for a "tuckar," the bracelet made of boar tusks worn by warriors before headhunting,

he didn't miss a beat: "Yeah, I've got one of them." I gave the matter no more thought and went with Francis to our quarters to sleep off the effects of the afternoon's meat and drink. Several hours later, as we were preparing to settle in for the night, the teenager suddenly rejoined us with a triumphant smile on his face. I challenged his claim to have real headhunter artifacts, to which he replied with a dramatic flourish, pulling out a superb "tuckar" from beneath his jacket. He waved it around and tossed it disdainfully to the ground at my feet; the tusks rattled the floorboards upon impact. I apologized profusely, being over eager and unable to restrain myself. He easily got his price: enough money for a large bag of rice for the coming winter. The bracelet was a beautiful armband made from two tusks of a wild boar, with the thick black hair of a headhunting victim hanging from the bone. Never again would I openly doubt the claims of the natives!

The "tuckar": headhunting ritual armband, with the hair of a headhunted victim attached to boar tusks, collected in Tulgao

Francis then rushed me to the hut of "Lumatac." This headhunter exhibited the same torso tattoo I had seen and photographed in Ambato. The warrior looked to be in his sixties, but though his face was timeworn and scarred, he kept fit with a strenuous regimen of hunting and gathering. He wanted to sell several headhunting axes. Because he wore the prized "fatoc" tattoo on his chest, indicating he had actually taken heads, I was inclined to accept the authenticity of his wares. After selling me an ax, we agreed to spend the following day together, and in a short while a genuine and respectful friendship developed between us.

"Lumatac" ate rice and waited for his wife to return home after her day of gathering in the jungle

In Lumatac, I had encountered a man of undeniable integrity, and I expressed unfeigned admiration for his strength and serenity. Lumatac told me only a warrior who had taken heads had the privilege of wearing the "fatoc" chest tattoo; anyone daring to display it without having actually taken a head would be laughed at and publicly ridiculed. Over the next week, I had the privilege of photographing one of the last remaining Kalinga headhunters.

The house we slept in that night was a sizeable dwelling, but all of us — the host family, my guide and myself — slept in the same room. I was unable to fall asleep as the noisy rites of passage and rituals continued just outside our front door. All night long, gongs rang out, chants and songs were repeated in lengthy cycles, as the men danced in a pulsating circular pattern. Using crude megaphones, the elders barked loud warnings, concerning the many responsibilities and trials of manhood, to the younger generation. My innocent expectation of an idyllic jungle retreat was shattered by the nightlong cacophony. The raucous commotion of the non-stop nocturnal celebration were punctuated throughout the night by the crying of my host's infant sons and the calm, soothing ministrations of their mother.

"Lumatac" prepared our meals over an open fire after he labored in his rice terrace and hunted in a nearby jungle.

Lumatac's survival depends upon his ability to successfully hunt and gather. He augments what he procures in the jungle, with rice he cultivates on terraces. His responsibility to the tribe, as a headhunter warrior and the status it carries, is an additional occupation he elects to bare. His "fatoc" chest tattoo insignia can be equated with our Western culture's military medals. The "fatoc" is a symbol of authority and rank, within the hierarchy of the village.

Fishing in the Chico river

Pausing on a hunt

Bathing in the Chico river

Eating from a coconut shell bowl

Gathering with a double sided basket

Sharpening a machete for clearing the jungle

Cooking at dusk

Cultivating a rice terrace

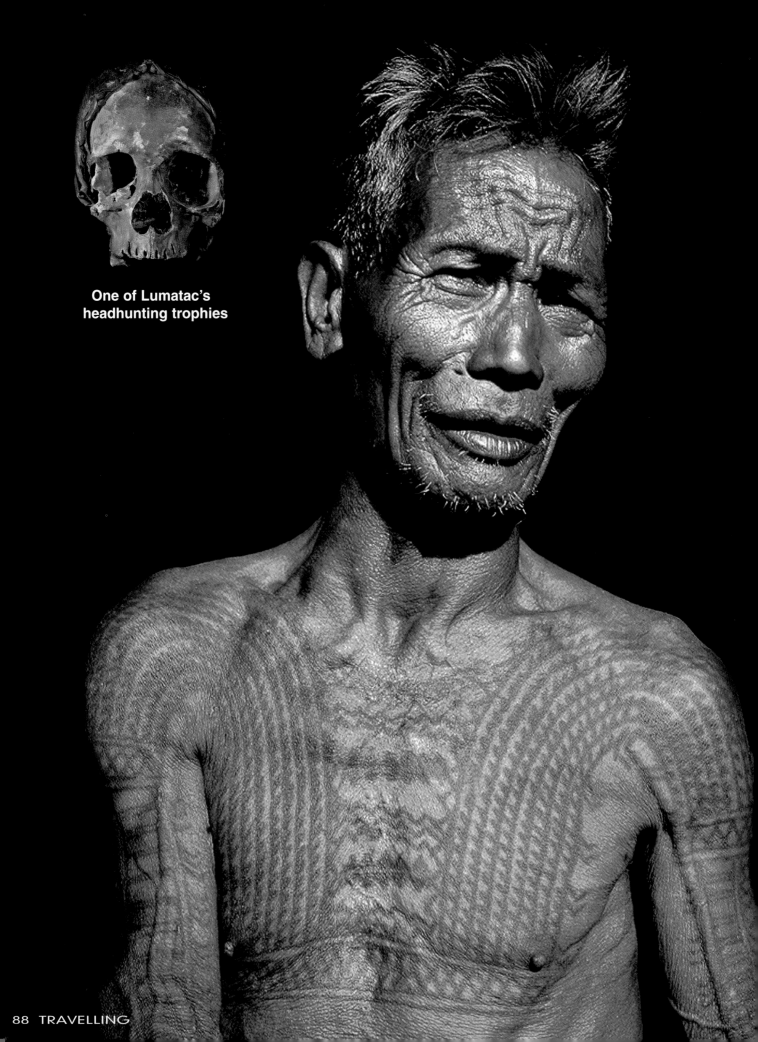

One of Lumatac's
headhunting trophies

After two days of being held up by continual rain, we decided to move on to the village of Bot-Bot. With Francis translating, I reluctantly said farewell to Lumatac and opened up my feelings: "I will always remember you and the hospitality you have shown me. You have taught me many valuable lessons, things you have always understood but I have never known. Perhaps your Kalinga ways are better for the spirit than those of my people." He seemed proud and even moved by my words, and replied: "Goodbye, my new friend. Come back if you can. You are American and I am Kalinga," he concluded, "but in my heart we are all of the same tribe." He never said another word. He just sat there. I took this final picture, as the light began to fade. I turned and regretfully left a noble dying breed: one of the last surviving Filipino headhunters.

"Malong": the young Kalinga female in Bot-bot, with the "linglingo" fertility charm her brother gave me.

After leaving Tulgao, my guide and I followed a circular route through Bot-bot and Ngibat, then finally returned to Tinglayan, which like Bontoc is the hub for outlying villages. Arriving in Bot-bot, I discovered the most complete and authentic traditional architecture of any Kalinga village I had yet seen. I set out to explore the village, and my eyes settled first on the main square of the village, where a large field of marijuana was growing, seemingly unattended. While Francis and I rested alongside the pot field, an attractive young Kalinga girl approached us. Barely adolescent, Malong embodied the Kalinga ideal of female beauty, clad in her traditional "ai-in" skirt and short yellow blouse. She stared at me with her large brown eyes and introduced herself in a friendly manner. She spoke a little English and knew Francis slightly, but quickly turned her attention to me: "I Malong. This my place and you are welcome."

very happy see new face with Francis. What call you?" I smiled and told her my name, which she repeated and asked, "You want go? You want go ere?," pointing to a nearby elevated hut. "We go!" I followed her up a ladder and found myself in a room stacked from floor to ceiling with drying marijuana. Malong opened an old wooden trunk in the corner, and withdrew a large bundle wrapped in old newspaper. She unwrapped the bundle slowly, revealing a dark brown block which she explained was hashish, the highly refined extract of the marijuana plant.

I followed her out of the hut and watched her distribute small chunks to all the assembled villagers, who eagerly stuffed it in their pipes and smoked it with glee.

After nearly half an hour of smoking, several of the natives began to behave erratically: one young man seemed to egress into an archaic animal form, baying at the blazing sun as if it were an enemy. Several of the intoxicated natives tried to speak to me, but none spoke enough English to make themselves clear. Every time I spoke to them, they would mimic me in their Kalinga dialect, as if they understood what I had said. I looked around and saw Malong beckoning from across the square, urging me to follow her again. She called out, "Come here?"

**The "O-kong" bachelor's hat
Malong gave to me in Bot-bot (top)
The Kalinga village
of Bot-bot (bottom)**

"You come! You come here!" My curiosity got the best of me and I followed her along a narrow path through several clearings, then down a steep hill leading away from the village. I felt like I was chasing a wild animal, a swifter creature who could maintain the distance between hunter and prey with ease. I finally realized we were heading in the direction of a small stream with a lone wood and straw hut standing nearby. I stood and watched her climb the ladder from a short distance away, fearful of being pulled into another marijuana storehouse, but when I finally climbed the steps and entered the hut, I found her innocently offering herself to me. She was far too young I decided. I was also not sure if the rest of the tribe would accept the idea of Malong and I being lovers. So I graciously declined, while making sure not to offend her. As we walked back to the village to try to find Francis, she presented me with a small round hat, decorated with a broad red band and boar tusks on either side. She took great delight in informing me the hat was a sign of my bachelor status. The hat appeared otherwise non-functional, but she explained Kalinga men also used them as a carrying pouch for nuts, money, cigarettes, and other valuables. Malong's brother; Guema was also benevolent. He extended friendship, and bestowed a gift upon me, of an

Malong and her brother held hands in vigil when I left their village of Bot-bot

The trail leading to Ngibat crossed over some of the most difficult terrain on the journey

extraordinary "linglingo" fertility charm he acquired on a trading sojourn to Bontoc. I placed my extensive supply of box matches inside my new hat, reasoning it might be better to take off a small, friendly little hat rather than open a large bag of goods and cameras, particularly when negotiating with the armed tribesmen who always stop outsiders, expecting tribute in exchange for the right to cross their territory. I wanted to

Worn by both men and women: the "linglingo" and "lufay" fertility charms are stylized representations of the female clitoris

The Ngibat females stretched their earlobes almost to their shoulders...

...wore raincoats made of straw, and smoked cigars in pipes

spend more time with Malong, but Francis seemed nervous about being in some way responsible for our budding relationship, and at his insistence we prepared to leave. The exhausting uphill morning hike from Tulgao to Bot-bot was more strenuous than my usual regime. Even before the day was half over the thin mountain air fueled a feeling of delirium. Francis sensed the situation, and offered to carry my cameras. I tried to give Malong a parting kiss, but she turned her head shyly. At a loss for words, I took a Thai silver bracelet off my wrist and silently gave it to her. She gazed back up again, imploring me with her mahogany brown eyes, with regret I turned and slowly walked away. Francis took the last picture of Malong holding her brother's hand. They both looked on, as I climbed the rocks alone leading to the jungle mountain trail. My next stop was the nearby village of Ngibat, where in comparison to Malong, beauty paled. The Ngibat village women's ears hung down almost to their shoulders; their earlobes stretched into a pendant form.

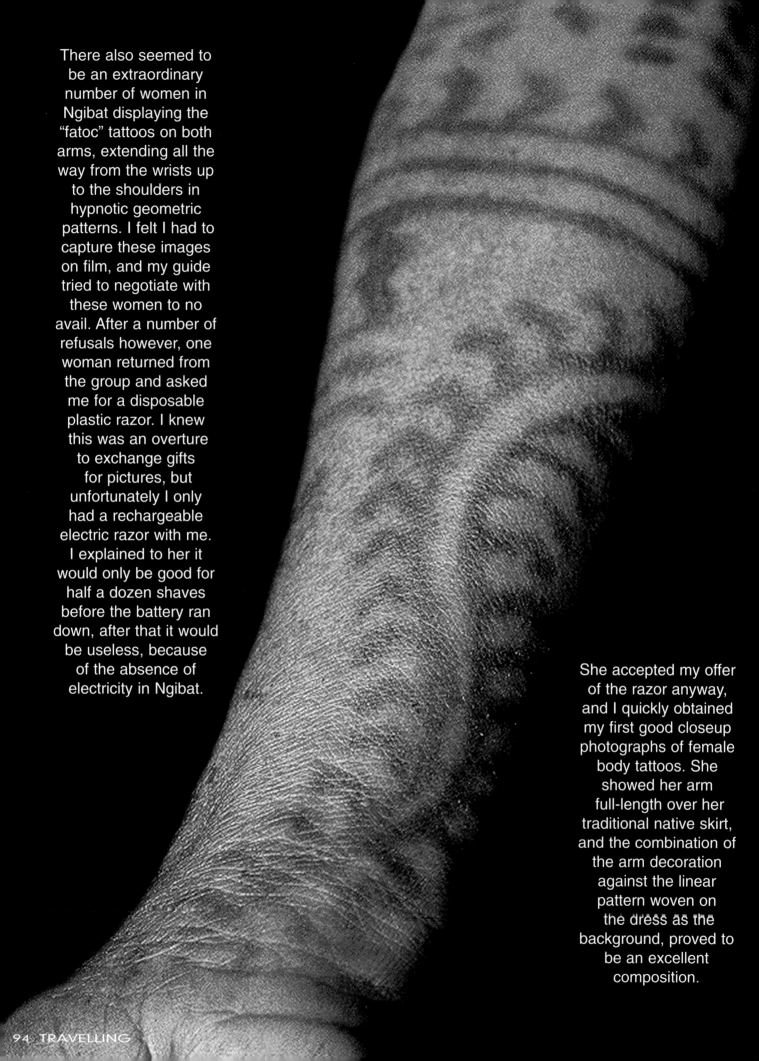

There also seemed to be an extraordinary number of women in Ngibat displaying the "fatoc" tattoos on both arms, extending all the way from the wrists up to the shoulders in hypnotic geometric patterns. I felt I had to capture these images on film, and my guide tried to negotiate with these women to no avail. After a number of refusals however, one woman returned from the group and asked me for a disposable plastic razor. I knew this was an overture to exchange gifts for pictures, but unfortunately I only had a rechargeable electric razor with me. I explained to her it would only be good for half a dozen shaves before the battery ran down, after that it would be useless, because of the absence of electricity in Ngibat.

She accepted my offer of the razor anyway, and I quickly obtained my first good closeup photographs of female body tattoos. She showed her arm full-length over her traditional native skirt, and the combination of the arm decoration against the linear pattern woven on the dress as the background, proved to be an excellent composition.

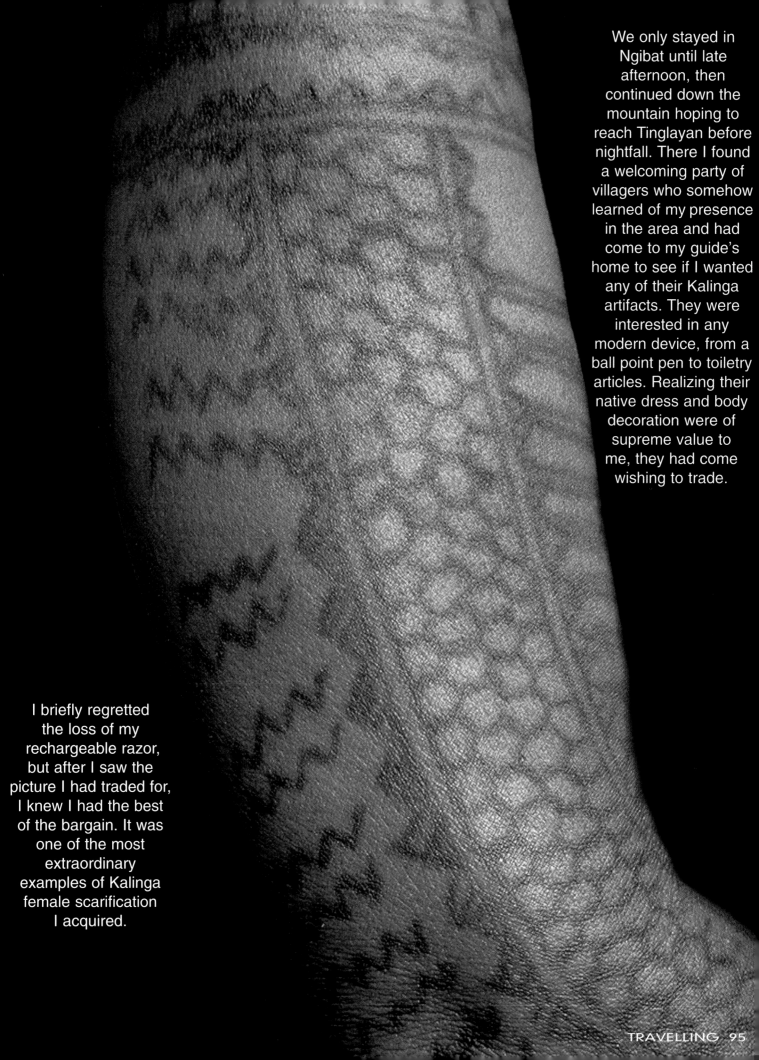

We only stayed in Ngibat until late afternoon, then continued down the mountain hoping to reach Tinglayan before nightfall. There I found a welcoming party of villagers who somehow learned of my presence in the area and had come to my guide's home to see if I wanted any of their Kalinga artifacts. They were interested in any modern device, from a ball point pen to toiletry articles. Realizing their native dress and body decoration were of supreme value to me, they had come wishing to trade.

I briefly regretted the loss of my rechargeable razor, but after I saw the picture I had traded for, I knew I had the best of the bargain. It was one of the most extraordinary examples of Kalinga female scarification I acquired.

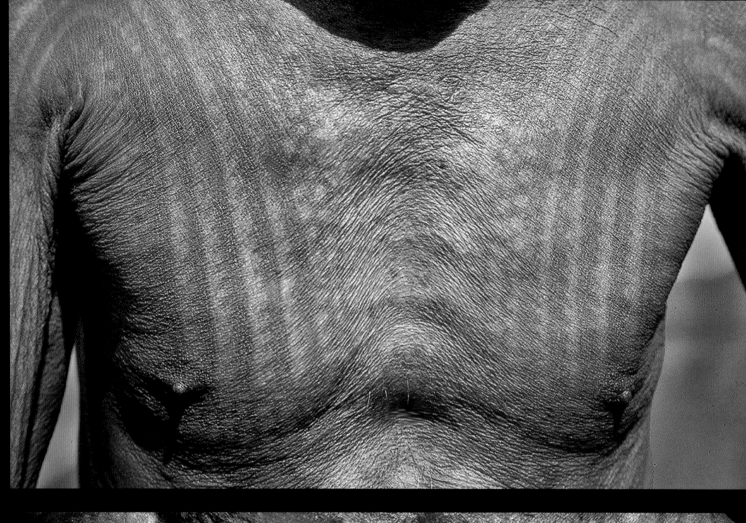
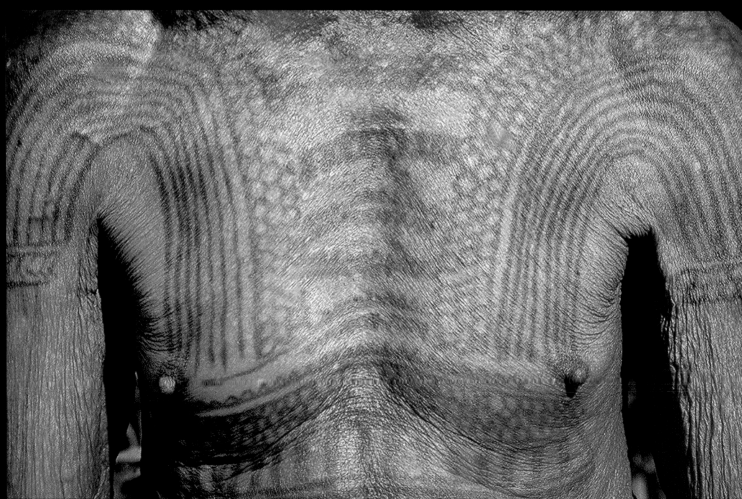

Four Kalinga headhunters from the villages of Tinglayan, Tulgao, and Bot-bot.

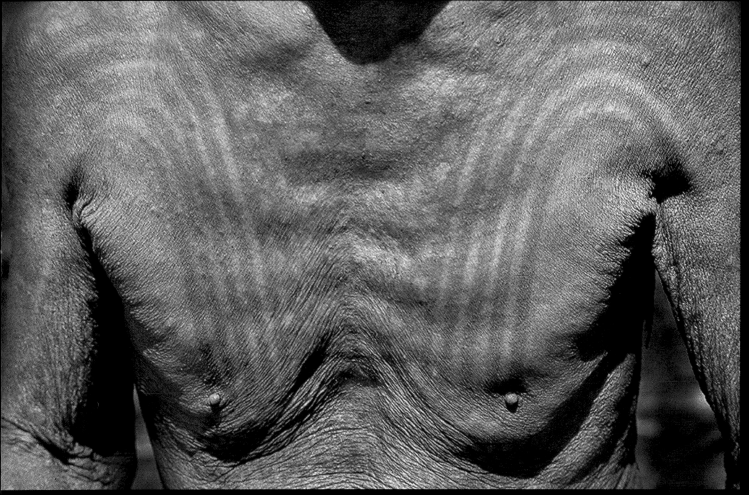
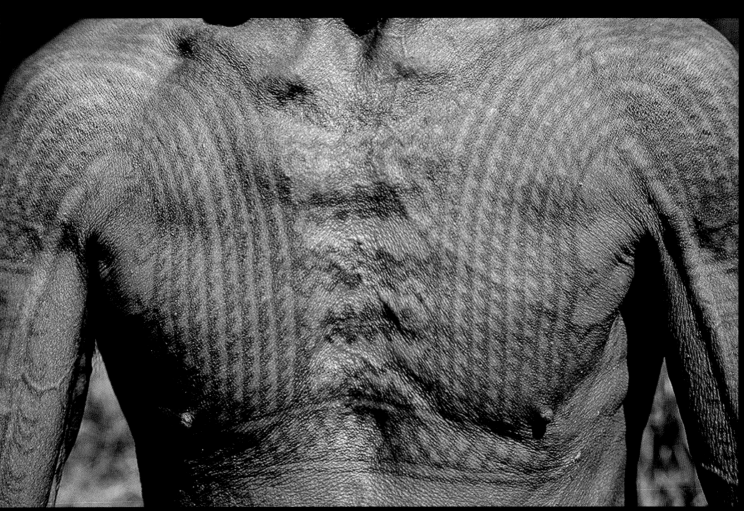

The "fatoc" chest tattoo, displayed only by warriors, is a tribal status symbol.

Soon I found three more men, with the body tattoos of a headhunter, and two women in full traditional dress, exhibiting body scarification. The women were bare-breasted, proudly showing their tattoos, and the men were eager to talk about their headhunting experiences, so I decided to stay on a few more days. The last artifact they offered me was a shiny human jawbone, used as a ritual gong handle, acquired in the nearby village of Basao. I was told it had been brought back from a successful headhunting raid, and asked to see the man who had returned with this prize. The original owner was "Puyao", a wizened old man proudly bearing the "fatoc" tattoo signifying the taking of a head. "I am eighty three years old, and I have taken twelve heads in the Kalinga villages of Tubuk, Lubuagan, and Basao." He not only knew exactly how many heads he had taken, he also knew the number of his people lost to rival tribes.

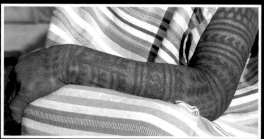

"Razor trade" picture (above),
"Owong": Kalinga female
(top three pictures),
Headhunting trophy
(bottom left)

"Puyao's" ritual jaw bone trophy
(facing page center)

"Yaing": Kalinga female, "Puyao" with
victims' jaw bones and hair, "Istak":
Kalinga headhunter, "Daging": and his
"chak-lang fatoc" headhunter's tattoo
(facing page clockwise from top left)

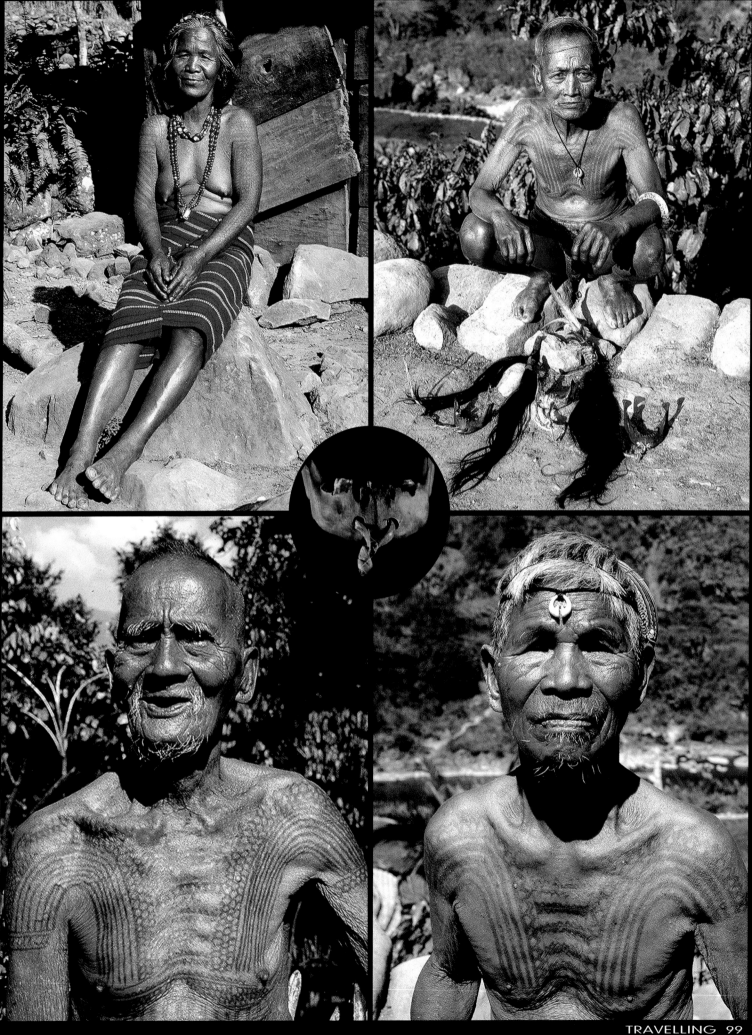

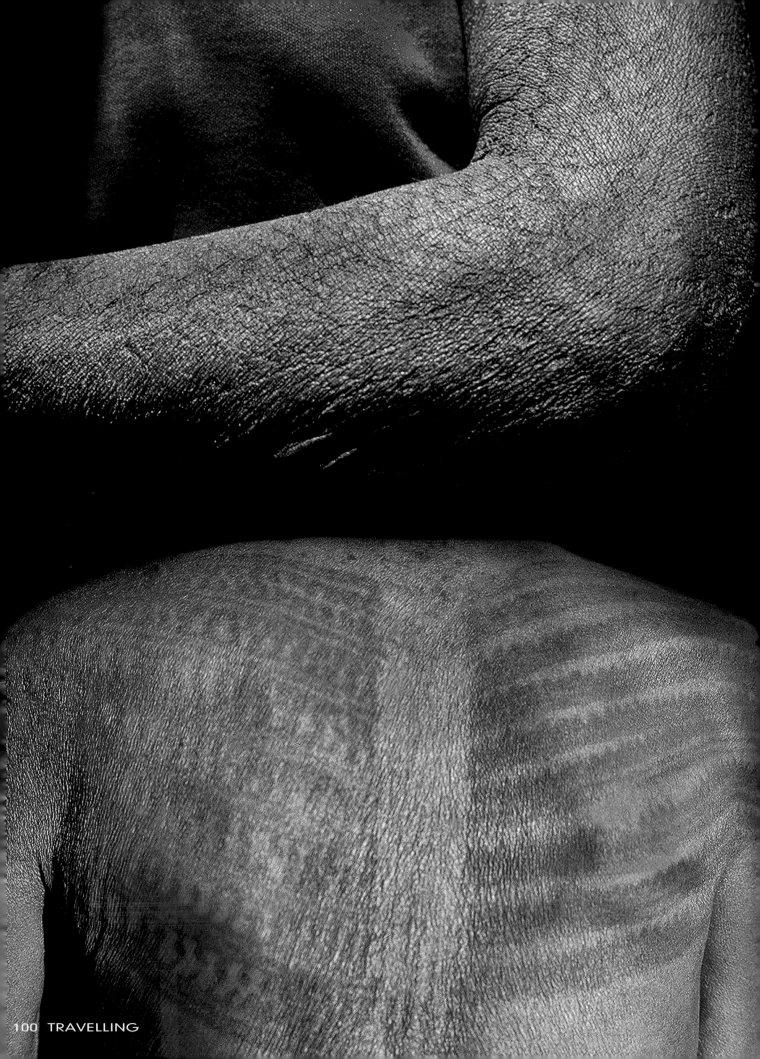

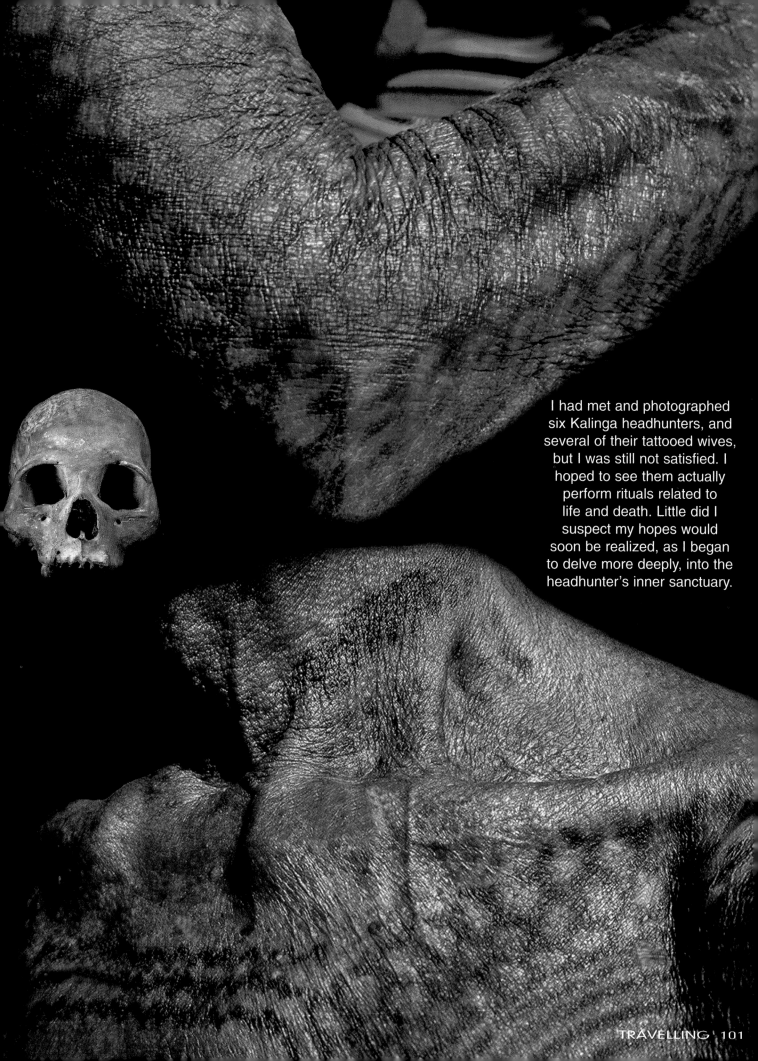

I had met and photographed six Kalinga headhunters, and several of their tattooed wives, but I was still not satisfied. I hoped to see them actually perform rituals related to life and death. Little did I suspect my hopes would soon be realized, as I began to delve more deeply, into the headhunter's inner sanctuary.

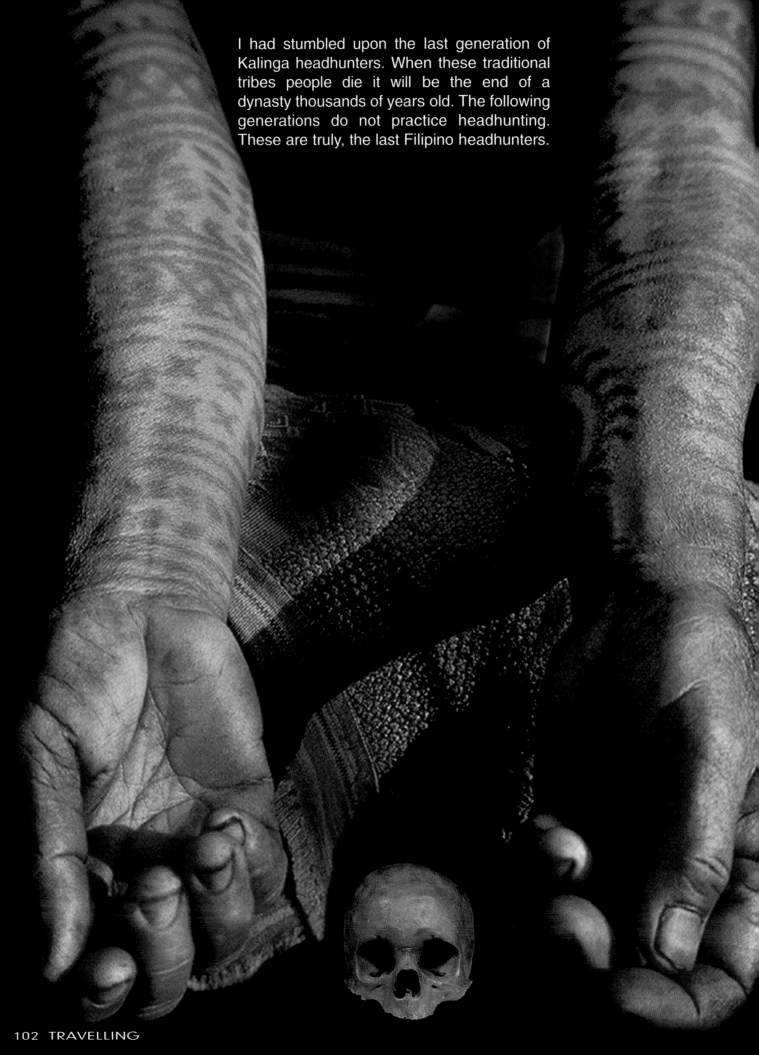

I had stumbled upon the last generation of Kalinga headhunters. When these traditional tribes people die it will be the end of a dynasty thousands of years old. The following generations do not practice headhunting. These are truly, the last Filipino headhunters.

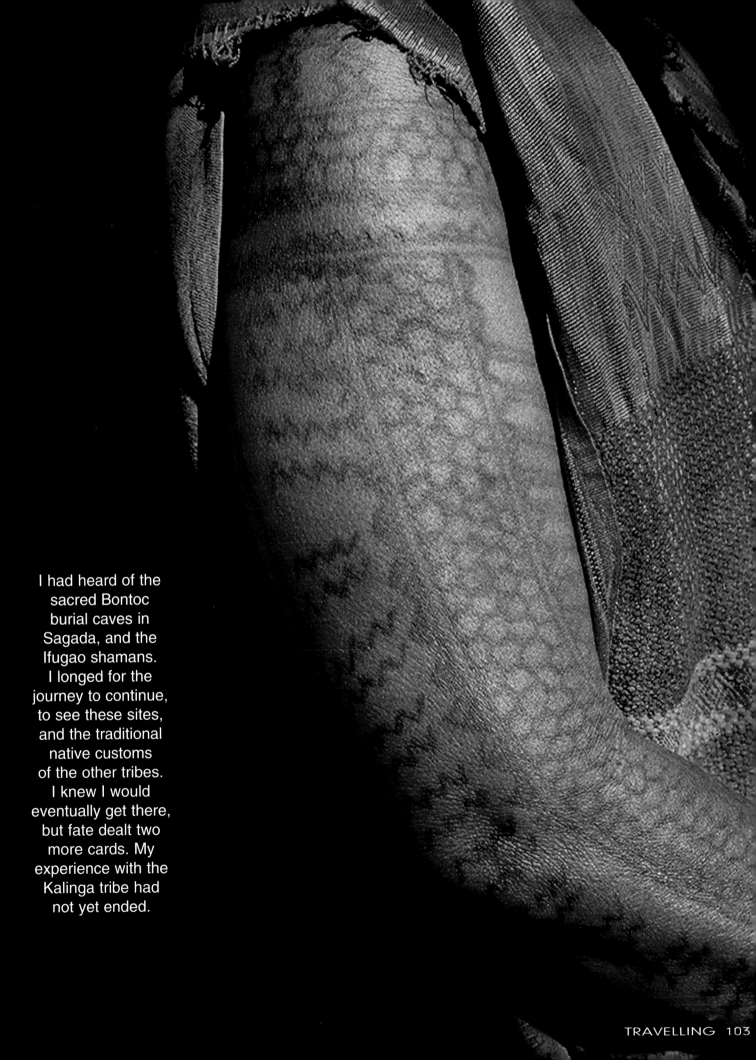

I had heard of the
sacred Bontoc
burial caves in
Sagada, and the
Ifugao shamans.
I longed for the
journey to continue,
to see these sites,
and the traditional
native customs
of the other tribes.
I knew I would
eventually get there,
but fate dealt two
more cards. My
experience with the
Kalinga tribe had
not yet ended.

"Owong-Ayyag"

I finally finished the extensive interviews and photographs of the Kalinga head hunters and their wives. I subsequently followed "Owong-Ayyag" a Kalinga female, for just a day, observing her daily activities such as, pounding rice, cooking, washing clothes in the river, basket weaving and smoking her ubiquitous tobacco pipe. After documenting her adorned body, I began to wonder if there was a reason for her tattoos! She suggested to me the tattoos are not only decorative, but also act as a means of identification, if she falls victim to a head hunter. Her body could easily be recognized by the other members of the village, after finding her decapitated remains. I then understood, how beauty is intricately woven into the Kalinga identity.

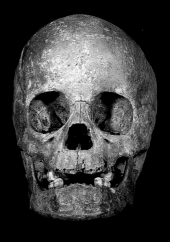

Owong collected coffee in the jungle and brought it back to the village in enormous one hundred pound sacks. She cleaned the beans in flat baskets and then she would barter the coffee in the nearby towns for matches, salt, flour, and all the other essential staples. When I was with her, she would cook meals for me and even though she had very little food, she was always willing to share. After two days the food I had brought, and whatever Owong had ran out.

The rest of the time we were together we only drank coffee, because it was all we had left. Our spirits never waned however. Just being together was enough. Even without food my excitement focused through my camera lens, onto her life and the tribe's customs. Owong was genuinely pleased with my interest in the heritage and the traditional ways of her village. It was difficult for me to separate myself from her when it was time to go. I felt as if I was leaving my mother, who I had only met once, and would never see again!

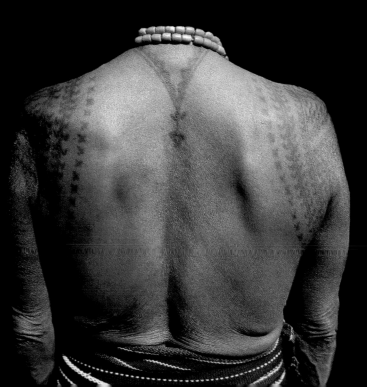

I had experienced
a day in
the life of a
headhunter's wife.

As Owong and I walked up to the road from the river, a jeepney to Bontoc came lurching around the bend o
an unscheduled run. I took this as a sign I should pack my bags. The driver waited patiently as I gathered a
my new found artifacts. Francis and I set out next for Bugnay, a village that lay back on the other side of th
Chico river, along the road back to Bontoc. Bugnay was accessible only by a precarious monke
bridge of hanging ropes, crossing which is an adventure in itself. Along the trail, after the crossing, w
encountered twelve heavily armed men walking single file, eleven with spears and one with a rusty M-1

The trail to Bugnay's "monkey" bridge

They allowed us to continue through their territory for the modest price of a single filter cigarette each. The group informed us they were on their way to a funeral in Bugnay, and would probably be seeing us again, no doubt in order to procure more cigarettes. Upon arriving in Bugnay I was immediately greeted by the Barangay Captain; the leader of the village. He was attired in Western casual wear, with a button down dress shirt, and tennis shoes. He told me in perfect English: "you are required to pay an entrance fee of 50 pesos ($2 US) before entering Bugnay." I paid the price and was allowed to enter the village with my guide Francis, who being Kalinga, was not charged admission. Upon arriving in Bugnay, late that afternoon, the first villager I encountered was a lovely young mother suckling a newborn. Captivated by her youth and beauty, I perhaps seemed overeager, for she rebuffed my repeated requests to take her picture.

The Kalinga village of Bugnay

This would have been an ideal image: a woman breast feeding the final generation of traditional Kalinga life, but in my haste I lost a golden opportunity to capture a fleeting glimpse into the simple values and innocence of a fast-fading culture. In my mind, this was the last mother to nurture an infant in the vanishing Kalinga tribe. The funeral we had been told about however, was under way and I was allowed to view the tribal ritual before the burial. The young man of about twenty, had suffocated from chronic tuberculosis, still an epidemic disease in the villages. The deceased had been an orphan without any surviving kin, but the villagers and their neighbors were mourning his death with a ritual sacrifice anyway. The village funeral custom followed a closely prescribed sequence of events, beginning with the deceased being placed sitting upright in a chair, to be observed and visited one final time

The Bontoc stop over on the way to Sagada's sacred burial caves

The head was held up by a cloth sash placed through the open mouth and tied to the back of the sea
holding the corpse in place. The purpose of the position was not to feign life, but to allow the mourners to se
the deceased more easily during the funeral rites, so as to directly address their parting love. During th
funeral, I was asked to supply some kind of alcoholic beverage, preferably gin, for the wake. Unprepared fo
this request, I hesitated to enter the inner sanctuary where the funeral was taking place, lest I risk a seriou
breach of Kalinga social etiquette. It was getting late, and Francis did not want to spend the night in Bugna
without a host, so he urged our departure. Fearing we would miss the last jeepney for Bontoc, we raced bac
across the rope bridge and scrambled, up the bank on the other side of the river, to the main road. W
waited most of the afternoon in the burning tropical heat, but no jeepney appeared. Stranded an
vulnerable in this strange foreign place, we could only camp by the roadside, but neither Francis nor I wer
comfortable without provisions. I passed a sleepless night recalling the ominous warnings I had heard abou
the Kalinga. At dawn, the arrival of the day's first jeepney felt like the welcome arrival of a long overdue frienc
I rubbed my eyes in happy disbelief as the driver pulled up twenty yards away and beckoned to us, anxiou
to procure two more paying passengers. The ride from Tinglayan to Bugnay, and now onto to Bontoc withou
having slept was exhausting, but I needed to catch a lift out of Bontoc to get to Sagada before dark. If I mad
it to Sagada by nightfall it would mean I had traveled continuously for more than thirty six hours. Glancing a
my watch, as we passed the boundary road marker separating the Kalinga and Mountain Provinces, I
decided it would be possible to get to Sagada and the burial caves before sundown. The anticipatio
of seeing the sacred burial sites keep me going, even though I had suffered through a sleepless nigh

My fellow jeepney
passengers from
Kalinga to Sagada

It was time for me to continue the journey, but I was reluctant to part company with Francis, who had proven to be a trustworthy guide and a loyal friend. I would be traveling alone from this point on, as my able Kalinga guide would be of little help in Bontoc territory. I felt a little lost as I watched him trudge off in the waning evening light, heading back to his home in Kalinga. It turned out to be unnecessary to search for a ride, since the first Bontoc storekeeper I came across ran a hotel in Sagada and offered to drive me there as soon as he got off work. The merchant made a jeepney run back to his home in Sagada every day

The jeepney stop in Sagada (left)

Sagada's limestone burial cave cliffs (above and facing page bottom left)

The town of Sagada (facing page bottom right)

at quitting time, and after recruiting more passengers by cruising up and down the streets frenetically honking his horn, he finally left Bontoc when every seat was occupied. By the time we reached the edge of the town, the jeepney was crammed, and conversation became almost impossible. At the first trestle bridge crossing the Chico river a police road block was stopping every vehicle. Half a dozen men in faded green camouflage with bolt action single shot rifles slung over their shoulders blocked the road. An infantryman approached, ordered us out of the car, and then led us over to a group of khaki-clad officers who proceeded to unpack and inspect our baggage. I looked in dismay at my scattered but unharmed belongings and artifacts,

Christian cemetery ritual grave fires in Sagada

until one of the officers barked impatiently, "You pack it back up!" He directed us back to the jeepney after this quick but thorough search, and once we were under way I asked the old man seated next to me why they had searched us. As he sat holding his precious supply of store-bought tobacco from Bontoc, he replied simply, "They search for those who travel from Kalinga." I didn't understand what he ment, but he went on to explain the soldiers were looking for drug runners carrying the renowned Kalinga marijuana and hashish. The government had been unable to locate the main source in the interior, and found it easier to intercept the runners at random roadblocks and regular checkpoints. As we entered Sagada, I looked up the narrow, winding road to the mountains.

An ancient coffin made from a hollowed tree trunk

Sagada is one of the most sacred locations in all the Philippines, and in recent years it has become an artists' colony and haven for expatriates from all parts of the globe. As I stepped down from the jeepney I looked at a "Lonely Planet" guide book map and immediately walked toward the nearest burial site, but I soon realized I would need a guide after all, since the caves looked too dangerous for me to explore by myself. I asked around for an experienced cave guide and was directed to "Rosie"; an eighteen year old girl. I was dubious about her abilities, but was assured she was the best guide in Sagada, her father having been a pioneer in exploring and mapping the caves.

I saw a blazing inferno in a Christian cemetery. Hundreds of graves had several fires burning on top of each burial mound directly in front of every tomb stone. I asked the jeepney driver if he knew the point of the burning tombs. He replied: "It's the Day of the Dead, once each year the Christians remember their ancestors and try to renew their forefathers' spirit with the ritual fires." I had not come to Sagada to experience esoteric Christian rituals, but rather to see the burial caves of ancient headhunters. The extraordinary circumstance of coming into contact with this Christian ceremony intrigued me, but my attention could not be diverted. Even though it was almost dark I set out to find the cave grave sites of the pagans I had traveled all night and day to photograph and explore.

The entrance to "Matang Kim" sacred burial cave in Sagada

Rosie warned me the caverns were too dark and dangerous for novices, but she entered them with only an old Coleman lantern and a long, heavy rope. I followed her down the pitch-black passageways, fearful she might drop our only light source into the underground river below. In the chilly darkness, I realized I would have to return again at dawn if I wanted to photograph the coffins, said to be stacked like cordwood within the caves. The early morning was the only time enough natural light penetrated the deepest interior; when my film would definitely be given the exposure it required.

Desecrated burial coffin, with hips and legs protruding

That night, I set my battery-operated alarm for 3:30 a.m. in hopes of catching the optimum conditions for photographing the entrance to the Matang burial cave. Setting out alone, I located a path leading around the side of a mountain, to a metal gate at the mouth of the cave. There were myriad dead-end channels and false entrances designed to confuse unwelcomed intruders. I entered and saw coffins stacked up on either side of a walkway, with an underground river running far below. Over millions of years, the water had carved out a gorge many hundreds of feet deep. The coffins rested on high ledges, balanced on either side along the walls of the cave, above the deep narrow river ravine.

After being diverted in the wrong direction by several confusing deceptions, I eventually located the actual cave entrance. I had to crawl through a tiny hole on my hands and knees, and after a half an hour struggle, I finally reached my goal: a spectacular collection of old coffins.

Lumiang cave: **stacked coffins** (facing page top and bottom left)
                      stacked coffins (above)
Matang Kim cave: **desecrated coffin** (facing page bottom right)
                      looking from inside out (top)
                      desecrated coffin with human remains (right)

I climbed up on a pile of rocks to position myself over the coffins for a better shot as the first light of day flooded the cave. I cocked the shutter, but my footing suddenly gave way as rocks broke loose. I tumbled down over the coffins, rolling to within a few inches of the dropoff to the river below. At the last second, the strap of my camera bag caught on one of the heavy wooden stakes used to keep the coffins closed. My fall was abruptly broken, and I lay with my head hanging over a decrepit coffin and my feet dangling out over the ravine. The strap gave way and I crashed down onto the casket, which lay perched on the edge of the precipice. There I lay hanging on for my life as the wooden lid cracked and broke open. I reached for another stake to hold on to, then swung my legs around and back onto the ledge. After a moment of desperate reflection on the irony of accidental death in an underground graveyard. I recovered my balance and slowly pulled myself away from the ledge. I stood up and found myself face to face with an intact

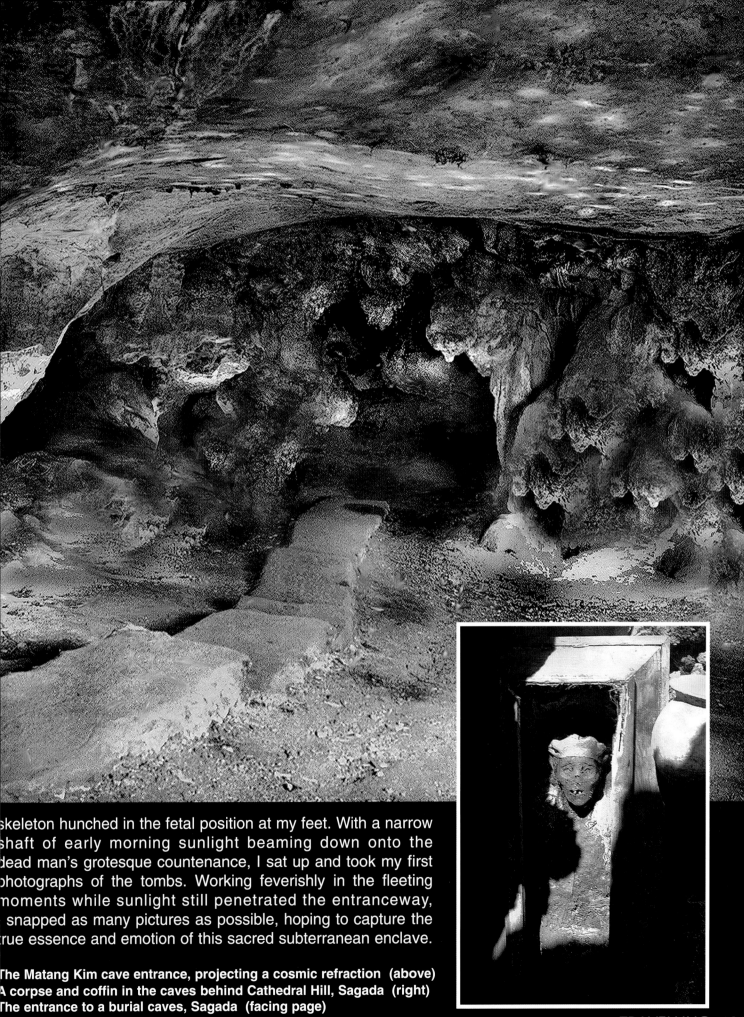

skeleton hunched in the fetal position at my feet. With a narrow shaft of early morning sunlight beaming down onto the dead man's grotesque countenance, I sat up and took my first photographs of the tombs. Working feverishly in the fleeting moments while sunlight still penetrated the entranceway, I snapped as many pictures as possible, hoping to capture the true essence and emotion of this sacred subterranean enclave.

The Matang Kim cave entrance, projecting a cosmic refraction (above)
A corpse and coffin in the caves behind Cathedral Hill, Sagada (right)
The entrance to a burial caves, Sagada (facing page)

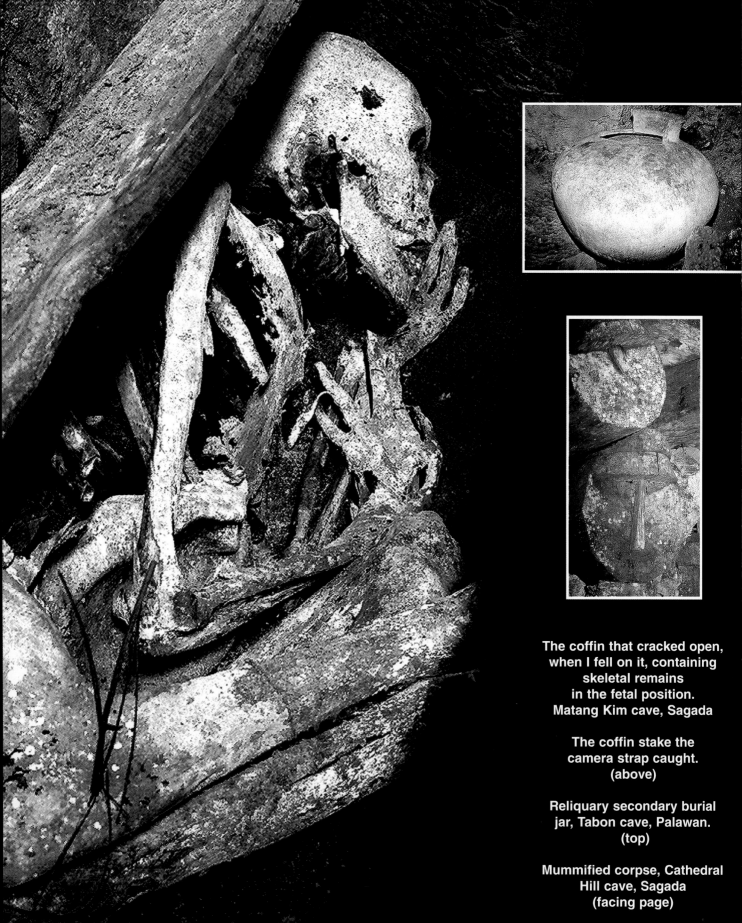

The coffin that cracked open,
when I fell on it, containing
skeletal remains
in the fetal position.
Matang Kim cave, Sagada

The coffin stake the
camera strap caught.
(above)

Reliquary secondary burial
jar, Tabon cave, Palawan.
(top)

Mummified corpse, Cathedral
Hill cave, Sagada
(facing page)

reluctantly returned to the mouth of the cave as the last light faded. At the entranceway, beams of sunlight reflected off of the gleaming mica cave floor and walls, refracting upward projecting hundreds of beads of light on the ceiling above, illuminating the cool darkness of the cave. It resembled a miniature cosmos. The unusual light refraction seemed to amplified the power contained within this consecrated spiritual domain. It is no wonder the tribes selected Matang Kim cave to celebrate the end of life, for their most beloved

Magnificent Ifugao rice terraces seen from Banaue's "Viewpoint"

The Ifugao town of Banaue

I was still determined, after seeing the Bontoc and Kalinga tribes, to explore all the major sites and to see villages from three tribal areas. A proper survey of Ifugao territory would complete my expedition, so I returned to Bontoc for a jeepney ride to Banaue, one of the principal towns in Ifugao province. The trip to Banaue took me down a bumpy dirt road, the tires churning up clouds of dust as I sped past small outposts and villages. The ride became even rougher as the road wound through the last mountain pass before Banaue.

The Ifugao Province, from the "Viewpoint", with the town of Banaue in the background

...ounding a sharp bend, I came to "The Viewpoint," a spectacular vista of the surrounding mountain peaks and the famous rice terraces. Road-weary and coated with dust from the trip, I stared wide-eyed in amazement at the dramatic landscape before me, then asked the driver to stop for a minute. I jumped from the truck and ran down an alleyway between two old wooden buildings, searching for the best possible view of the terraces stretching up the mountainsides to the summits. Walking around the corner while peering intently toward the horizon, I stumbled over a pair of wooden canes in the middle of my path. I picked myself up and there I met my first Ifugao, a tiny old woman sitting on a wooden crate. As I stammered a quick apology, she grasped her hand-hewn crutches and pulled herself up to her full height of less than four feet.

Ifugao at the "Viewpoint". "Lingayon" playing the flute. "Lingayon" with her hand made crutches (facing page)

"You are searching for something. But you have found something you were not looking for!", she said and introduced herself as "Lingayon." Her exotic ensemble consisted of a feathered headdress with an animal skull, brilliant white and multicolored beaded necklaces, and a tribal tunic with vivid orange and purple stripes. I asked what she was doing in this placc and she glanced down at a stack of neatly folded tunics similar to the one she wore. When I inquired if she had any older tribal clothing or textiles for sale, she pulled an antique Ifugao woman's "tapis" dress from her shoulder bag. The thread bare fabric had a geometric pattern I admired, but it had been patched in places and she quickly agreed on a price. I wanted to stay and talk with Lingayon, but feared the jeepney driver would grow impatient and drive off with all my luggage. I began to leave, then turned back, took an impromptu photograph of her and raced back to the road.

The rice terraces surrounding the Ifugao town of Banaue

I climbed aboard the jeepney with my treasure under my arm
pleased with a transaction that had taken less than a minute
and dwelled upon the antique dress in silent satisfaction. The
the driver interrupted my revery as he jerked into gear and w
plummeted down the steep route to Banaue in the valley below.
eventually returned to the roadside overlook, and was delighte
to find that Lingayon was always there, waiting patiently at th
same location. My satisfaction at finding a fixed point of referenc
in the area was dampened by the realization that Lingayon'
immobility was the result of crippling ailments that prevented he
from leaving the vista point. After that, I made a point of goin
back to the overlook when I could, to take pictures of the ric

The Ifugao terraces are more than 3000 years old

terraces with the valleys below, and to buy one more of the colorful garments Lingayon had to offer. Everywhere I looked I saw artisans hard at work carving wood, fashioning baskets, and weaving textiles. I was impressed by the sophisticated level of the local artwork on display. If the Kalinga were the fiercest and the Bontocs the most civilized, the Ifugao were easily the eminent artists of the mountains. I was told in Sagada the Banaue museum had a major collection of artifacts from the surrounding villages, and that the display indeed embodied the artistic temperament of the Ifugao people. I instinctively felt I had at last found a spiritual home among the tribes. I went to the museum and found a funeral for William Beyer in progress.

The son of the noted German anthropologist Otley Beyer, had died, and a carabao cow was being sacrificed in his honor. Villagers from across the province had gathered in spite of a steady rain. We all lined up under the long overhanging eaves of the museum outbuildings, huddling together to keep dry as the rain began falling harder. When the enormous bolo machete cut through the animal's neck, blood poured down the hillside, mixing with the runoff and forming a bright red stream of viscous fluid which flowed through the rock-lined drainage ditches. This dramatic ceremony was a fitting tribute to a man who had spent his entire life in the service of the Ifugao people. I was eager to photograph the ritual, but my shutter jammed in the extreme humidity of the tropical downpour. As I fumbled with my camera, William Beyer's son Henry ntroduced himself, while questioning me about my technical problem. I offered my condolences, and he assured me there would be more sacrifices honoring his father, one every day for the next week. As in the Kalinga village of Tulgao, each one of the villagers was given a share of the slaughtered animal to take home. Some of the meat was cooked over an open fire pit dug in the dirt and shared among the mourners. While the meat broiled a bystander walked up behind me and inquired in English, "Looking at the food can make you hungry! Come, I invite you to eat in my village. Please, follow me." I turned around and faced an elderly man clad in peculiar attire: a crown-shaped hat, an elaborate loincloth, and a cape, all fashioned from a vivid fabric with vertical red and black stripes. "Thank you," I replied, "But I do not know where your village is or who you are." He introduced himself as "Mongit," leader of the nearby village of Tam-an, where he headed a clan of some twenty-five people.

"Mongit": the leader of the Ifugao village of Tam-an, with his wife and grand daughter.

I was suspicious of the old man at first, but soon realized my apprehension was unjustified and agreed to go with him. I followed him in silence to the edge of the town, where he turned down a path into the jungle. I looked at the ankle-deep mud from the runoff of the rice terraces, and briefly questioned my judgement before pursuing him down the trail. It took us only about twenty minutes to get to Tam-an. Small though it was, the cluster of seven or eight huts had electrical power, a luxury which Mongit's people attributed to his prowess as a leader. Mongit was as good as his word, and immediately upon our arrival his wife served us a fine meal. After dinner, he lit a cigarette from the embers of the fire and said softly, "I think maybe you have come a long way and seen many things, but I can also show you things here in Tam-an, things you have never seen before." I stayed in Mongit's village for a week, only returning the short distance to Banaue to buy gifts for Mongit's clan and supplies for myself. During my Tam-an sojourn, I had the pleasure of photographing the celebration surrounding the birth of a child, one of the wonders Mongit had been hinting at. Mongit's people danced happily as the musicians played the traditional brass gongs for the birth ceremony.

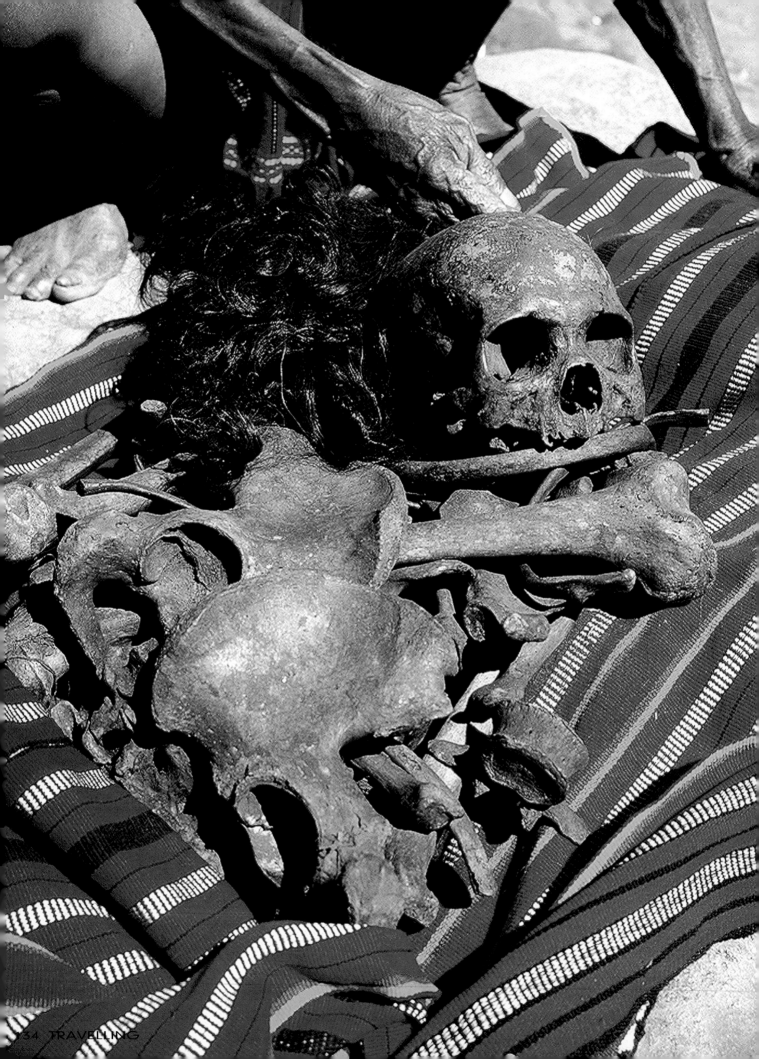

Mongit approached me quietly, his warm eyes shining brightly in his wrinkled brown face. The old man shyly asked if I would like to see his father. I assured him I did, expecting to meet an even older, more wrinkled patriarch. He turned and hobbled back toward his hut, an elevated structure on four tall tree stumps. He then bent down, reached under the floor near the entrance, and pulled out a rolled up blanket. Unfolding the blanket carefully, he revealed the bones of his dead father, heaped in a small pile with the skull and hair intact.

Mongit and the bones of his father, which he kept under the floor of his hut

After I photographed the honored ancestor, Mongit rewrapped the skeleton and returned it to the storage area under the floor of the hut. I looked more closely and realized there were half-a-dozen more blanketed skeletons stored alongside his father, all stacked neatly in a row. I then realized a deep concern for burial rituals and the preservation of the remains of the ancestors was a universal trait of the tribes in all three provinces I had visited. The Kalinga chose to bury their dead in the grounds around their huts in a kind of family cemetery; the Bontoc preferred a more formal ritual befitting the grandeur of the burial caves of Sagada and many of the

**Four generations of Tam-an Ifugao:
Mongit, the father's skeleton, and this family**

Ifugao, I now discovered, preserved their departed ones in storage racks under their living quarters, as if to emphasize the closeness of the ancestors to the living. If the spirits of the ancestors are needed to help perform a ceremony, the priests take the bundled bodies out from under the hut and display them before the assembled tribe, while chanting and summoning the spirits of the dead. Each village has its own variations on these basic burial methods, but the common quality to all the tribespeople was a physical intimacy with the remains of family members which disturbed my Western preconceptions of reverence for the dead.

Mongit became a close friend, and at the end of my visit to Tam-an he made the supreme gesture of offering me his personal pair of rice guardian figures, family heirlooms which he used in his role as Ifugao shaman when he performed the annual rice harvest benediction. "Take these as your remembrance," he said, handing me the small statues. I was reluctant to presume too much on his hospitality, but allowed my collector's instinct to overcome my better judgement, telling myself it would be impolite to decline such a generous gesture. After many declarations of friendship and good wishes, I left Tam-an that afternoon with my first authentic Ifugao ceremonial carvings. I walked back to Banaue along the same jungle path Mongit and I took to his village. The dripping humidity of the air made the tropical heat almost unbearable, but the path was dry and hard this time. After a few minutes of hiking at a steady pace, sweat poured down down my forehead and blurred my vision. I grew light-headed, and soon the winding jungle path was transformed into a whirling tunnel of color and sound. On the trail ahead, I seemed to see a tiny wood figure similar to the ones Mongit had given me. Convinced that I was hallucinating, I walked past the figure, then turned around to assure myself it was not real. But the little figure remained where I had seen it, when I bent down to touch it, my apparition proved to be solid and substantial. I held the little idol up in a shaft of light to examine it more closely, and to my amazement found it identical in every way to Mongit's. The figurine, my rational mind told me, must have been accidentally dropped by a passing Ifugao, but to my fevered imagination it seemed like a sign my journey was blessed by the tribal gods. Back in Banaue,

Mongit's gift: two sacrificial Ifugao "bulul" rice guardians

The tiny sacrificial "hipag bulul" found on the path

I checked into the "People's Lodge," where travelers gathered in the dining room nightly to swap stories and seek information. One night I ate dinner with two German men and one French girl named Marie. Although I was tired after a week in the jungle, I was intrigued by the description of a recent expedition to Batad; they declared it to be the most traditional and authentic of the Ifugao villages in their experience. I was relieved to learn the Ifugao were a gentle, friendly people, and I would require no guide on the easy-to-follow map and jungle route to Batad.

The next morning I hired a "tri-cycle," a motorcycle with a homemade sidecar heavily decorated with religious statuettes, bumper sticker prayers, and the vehicle's name painted garishly in big, bright letters on the roof. I spent the next two hours bouncing down a rough dirt road to Batad Junction, a turnout where a footpath led away from the road and straight up the mountainside. My driver assured me it would take no more than three or four hours of hiking to reach Batad. I started up the overgrown path, but within minutes encountered the young French woman Marie I had met the day before, waiting in a shed by the side of the mountain trail. She jumped up and embraced me happily, as if I had rescued her from some desperate plight, and at once we set off down the path arm in arm. After about two hours of climbing up the steep mountain trail my new traveling companion succumbed to the midday tropical heat and suddenly collapsed in a dead faint. I grabbed my plastic water bottle and splashed its precious contents on her face.

A "tri-cycle" dropped me off at "Batad Junction"

Huts in Batad, (above)
The Ifugao village of Batad (facing page)

Marie revived quickly, and we agreed to rest for half an hour before resuming the journey. When she felt better, however, she decided she would rather return to Banaue than continue climbing. It took me over an hour of pleading and promising to get Marie to agree to press onward. I had no wish to turn back at this point, but I was unwilling to abandon her in these unfamiliar mountain forests. Fortunately, my chivalrous instincts prevailed, and I settled on a solution that would allow me to keep my traveling companion and hold to my itinerary as planned. If she would let me carry her on my back to Batad, I would guarantee her safety and help her get back to Banaue in a few days. Marie hopped up piggy-back onto my shoulders and I lumbered up the hillside. The overhanging branches had obscured the trail ahead, and I was relieved to reach a clearing where I could see we were near the crest. After another twenty minutes of struggling, we finally reached the summit, where a sweeping panorama unfolded before us, stretching from the lush green mountain horizon down to Batad. The village appeared to be divided into several residential sections, encircled by a network of enormous rice terraces. Our spirits revived as our destination came into view. Marie no longer needed a native bearer and we marched down the mountain trail at a steady pace. Approaching the bottom of the mountain, we could see activity in the center of the village. When we reached the outskirts of the village I heard ritual chanting.

Voices repeating abstract sounds echoed in the enormous rice terrace mountain canyons surrounding the Ifugao village of Batad. As I consciously moved in the general direction of the voices I began to question if they did indeed existed, or was it merely my imagination reacting to extreme exhaustion. I asked Marie if she also could hear the voices, and she simply replied: "What voices!" Feeling threatened, my pulse rate increased with added adrenaline, while I lost faith in my ability to accurately perceive my surroundings. Then Marie anxiously screamed, "Wait, wait, wait, I do hear voices!"

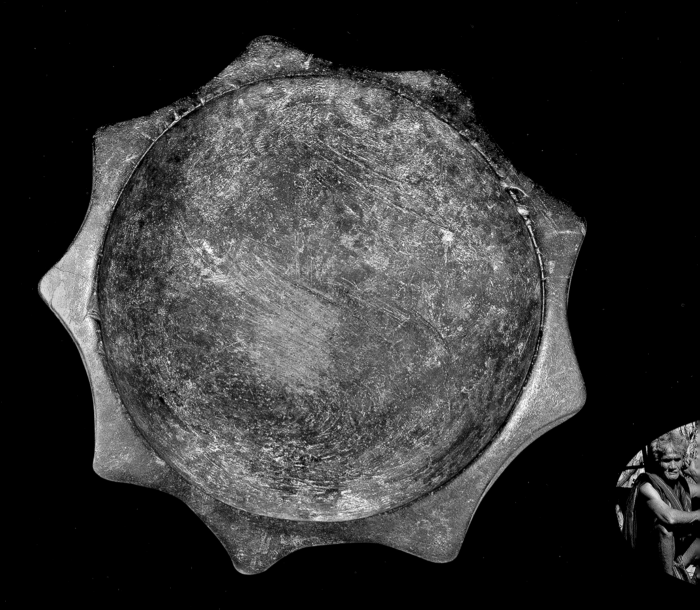

The star shaped "dinalo" wooden bowl is used in the Ifugao "canao" sacrificial ritual. (above)

The "canao" ritual, performed by shamans, determines the fate of the sick by sacrificing chickens and examining the color of the bird's entrails. (facing page)

We entered the village and soon encountered a group of traditionally dressed Ifugao man. They had just killed a chicken and were now inspecting the bird's entrails. We watched from a respectful distance as they probed the liver, laid it next to a wooden box on the ground and drew cups of rice wine from a star shaped bowl. Only then did they turn their attention to the unlikely pair of Western visitors staring at them. The boldest of the three, a short, slight man with a congenial smile and an affable air, approached us and introduced himself as "Gem-o". I asked him what they were doing, and he explained they were Mombaki priests doing "canao," the Ifugao ritual to cure sickness. I was interested in learning more about this primitive ritual, but Marie seemed more concerned with finding a place to rest and recuperate from the day's ordeal. I suggested she look for a guest house while I interviewed and photographed the three shamans. She agreed and headed off into the village. That was the last time I ever saw Marie. I never found out where she had gone or what had happened to her. Later I inquired at all four guest houses in Batad, but Marie was nowhere to be found. I was naturally very worried about her, but the shaman Gem-o reassured me with a strange little song: "Be happy in our ways, Be happy in our ways, She has nothing to fear here, So be happy in our ways!" The high priest's uplifting singsong chant entranced me and soon laid my fears to rest. I wanted to speak further with Gem-o, only to find he had lost interest in my dilemma and returned to his ritual. The priests seemed ill at ease performing chants and prayers in the presence of a stranger.

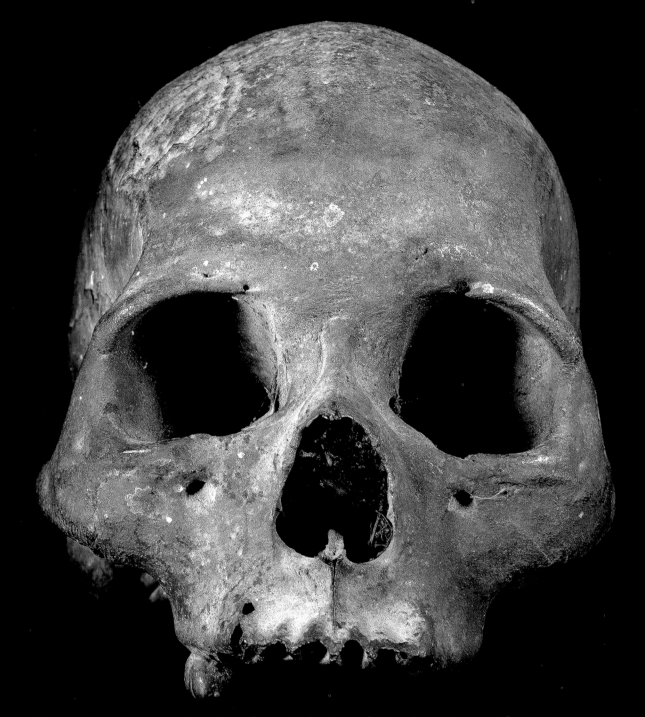

The trophy taken on a headhunting raid in the neighboring village of Cambulo (above)
Narcisco, the Ifugao shaman, holds the headhunting trophy at a "canao" healing ceremony (facing page)

Gem-o and the others continued with their "canao" ritual, bringing out another chicken for the sacrifice. The bird crowed several times, punctuating the ceremony, then gave a frightening last cry as it's throat was slashed. I discovered Gem-o was a layman most of the time, but as a Mombaki shaman he became a sanctified individual during the performance of the Ifugao canao ritual. As the ceremony proceeded, his demeanor changed and his very appearance was transformed; the Ifugao gods seemed to take possession of his spirit. He focused all his attention on the sacrifice of the chickens, draining the birds' blood and carefully examining their livers before revealing the patient's fate. After the sacrifice, the shamans seemed satisfied with the results. I was able to then draw them into a discussion about the various objects used in the ritual and ask if they had any artifacts to sell or trade. Without a word the second priest of the group, "Narcisco", walked off behind a nearby hut. He returned quickly with a package bundled in cloth, which he unwrapped to reveal a skull blackened with age. He said it was given to him by his father, who had been dead for more than forty years. The skull was taken on a headhunting raid in the neighboring village of Cambulo.

"Gem-o", the Ifugao Mombaki shaman took me hunting, because his wife had not returned from gathering food in the jungle.

Gem-o started a fire to cook the dead snake he found wrapped around a dead owl.   (left)

Hunting in the jungle around the Ifugao village of Batad.   (above and facing page top)

At night, after the evening meal, Gem-o was satisfied. (right)

Forgetting the inevitable problems I would have explaining this headhunting trophy to the U.S. customs inspectors, I accepted the Mombaki shaman's offer of his prized family heirloom. After Narcisco agreed to my purchase of the skull, Gem-o invited me to his hut for dinner. We walked a short distance down a hillside on a trail winding between the rice terraces and pockets of huts. At Gem-o's home, unfortunately, no food was on hand, so he proposed we go hunting instead; we would have to catch our dinner. He beckoned me to follow as he said, "Wife no come back. She went jungle for food. She no come back." Taken with the spontaneity of his suggestion, I followed the hunter-gatherer as he searched for food, carrying a spear, machete and rattan backpack. With his hunting dog at our side, we set off in quest of birds, lizards, wild pigs or any other game he might find. He foraged as he hunted, ever alert to the possibility of obtaining any foodstuff, even wild vegetation.

Gem-o searches the underbrush with a machete, hoping to gather food for our dinner

Over the next few days, he fashioned the vertebrae of the snake into a necklace, and turned the owl's wings, head and beak into an elaborate hat. By the end of the week, he was wearing this new garb during the performance of his priestly duties. On our way back, he picked up a large tree limb and threw it over his shoulder, balancing the heavy burden with his lance. He explained, "Fire! Cook! Eat snake! Me, you, with wood," indicating we would need the limb for fuel to cook our snakemeat dinner. Back at his hut, Gem-o cut up the snake, then took half the kill over to his neighbor. This magnanimous gift was reciprocated with a full bottle of the cheap local gin. Gem-o was delighted with this exchange, and began imbibing as he skewered the remaining snakemeat with a stick. He then set the meat on an impromptu barbecue spit over a bed of simmering coals left over from his morning fire. I was tired and hungry after a long day, and was actually grateful for the reptilian repast.

We searched the thick brush for hours until I grew exhausted and pleaded to return to his hut. He would not consider quitting so soon, and the hunt for food continued for several more hours, until at last we came across a small mountain spring. As he drank from the pool, he glanced up and spied a snake with a death grip around the neck of a predatory owl. Neither hunter nor prey could escape his adversary's stranglehold, and in death the two were bound together forever by the universal will to live. Gem-o quickly stuffed the two freshly-killed combatants into his pack and we headed back to his hut. He was particularly pleased to have gained his prey effortlessly, as he saw it.

Carrying the fire wood used to cook the snakemeat Gem-o with his owl hat, snake bone necklace, and divination effigies (facing page)

We drank the warm gin, chewed the half-charred snakemeat, and over time established a friendship that proved to be long-lasting and deeply rewarding. Before we fell asleep that first night, Gem-o informed me that in three days the annual "Mom-batak" harvest ritual would be performed. Having heard of this ritual, I looked forward to actually seeing it, but Gem-o said I could not attend the ceremony without a personal invitation from Nestor, the largest landowner in Batad. My disappointment lingered as I slipped off to sleep, vowing to pursue the matter the next day. The following morning, I asked Gem-o to take me to Nestor to see if I could attend the harvest ritual. After a few hours he relented and took me to a small cluster of huts closer to the center of the village. I had expected to see a fat, prosperous land baron, but instead found a groveling, disheveled figure who immediately began begging for gifts. When I demurred, he suggested I give him money for some type of ointment he needed. I approached cautiously. Nestor looked malnourished and sick, but I showered him with great respect

Gem-o introduced me as a traveller interested in Ifugao traditions. Leery of possible contagious disease, I kept my distance and told the land owner firmly: "Nestor, I respect your people and their customs. I have come to ask your permission to attend the rice harvest ritual. Please consider my reasons for wanting to attend the ceremony. I hope to record the ritual for historical purposes so your people's customs will live forever in the hearts and minds of all people everywhere." Nestor thought this over for a moment and replied, "You may attend the ceremony if you give to my people the pig and three chickens for our sacrifice." He assured me there would be plenty of music and dancing, and he would use all three of his bulul statues in the ritual. I accepted his terms too quickly, so he immediately raised his price by three quarts of gin. Suspecting his demands would escalate repeatedly in the days remaining before the ritual, I pulled out a ballpoint pen and a piece of paper from my pack and drew up a binding written agreement.

Nestor's "bulul" statue and "punamhan" sacrificial box, used in the rice harvest ceremonial ritual

I read it aloud as he nodded his acceptance, then I handed him the paper and asked him to put his mark or thumbprint in the lower right hand margin. Our initial agreement called for three dances, two sacrificial ceremonies (one for the pig and another for the chickens), and full musical accompaniment. But when I rubbed the ballpoint ink on his thumb and presented the contract for his mark, he at once demanded another 1,000 pesos in cash, sensing my determination to see the ritual. I acquiesced reluctantly, knowing I had no real bargaining power over the sickly old man. I was willing to meet all his terms if I could do so without being victimized, but I knew if I appeared too easy to exploit he would continue his demands indefinitely. As I left the grueling negotiation with Gem-o, I asked him why Nestor had so much control over the villagers. His house was an ordinary hut, his clothes were ragged and torn, and he showed no outward signs of status.

Gem-o, on the way to Nestors' (facing page)
Gem-o's ritual objects: necklace, wooden hat, pregnant female effigie, and ritual box (left)

Gem-o's reply was enlightening. "Nestor rich no more, but old ritual way same. Nestor still own father's land, but rice make money no more. Nestor must get harvest pig, but no have money like before." It seemed that Nestor's family had once been very wealthy. He still owned many rice terraces and the granary where the ceremony took place every year. Without his cooperation, there could be no harvest festival. I asked why he was so destitute, and Gem-o explained that Nestor was a victim

of changing times. The rice harvest could no longer support the growing population, and most of the food supply was now being carried in from Banaue on the backs of porters, over the same steep trail I had traversed with Marie. As a result, the value of the rice terraces had fallen sharply, and Nestor's considerable land holdings were no longer the main source of Batad's wealth. Poverty had greatly affected Nestor's mental condition, Gem-o said, and he

Gem-o presiding as a "Mombaki" shaman at the " Mom batak" harvest ritual

could no longer afford to provide the rice and animals for the sacrifice, even though it was his obligation. Nestor's plight was typical of the changing economic and social realities of the Ifugao world. As the largest landowner, he still was expected to pay for the ritual sacrifices, but he could no longer afford them. Nestor was literally impoverished by his obligations, and the shame of his inability to perform his hereditary role had broken his spirit and ruined his health. The rituals began as scheduled two days later anyway. I arrived at Nestor's with my camera and delivered the agreed-upon three bottles of gin,

having already paid Nestor for the pig and the chickens. I was to pay the last 1,000 pesos at the end of the ceremony if everything went well. Nestor's son and mother were in attendance, and Narcisco, Gem-o and three other priests began the rituals with a flourish. The sacrifice of the pig was carried out enthusiastically, the dancers moved to the rhythmic ringing of the gongs as I took pictures. After about an hour and a half, however, the consumption of the gin began to take its toll and the crowd grew drunk and unruly. In the midst of this alcohol fueled frenzy, Nestor suddenly approached and demanded another hundred pesos for each of the forty or more celebrants. My patience with Nestor's continually escalating demands was now at an end, and I calmly refused to meet any additional demands. I had seen only one ritual and one dance so far, and the intoxicated performers were making it almost impossible for me to work. I decided to cut my losses while I still had enough money left to return home. The crowd had plenty of food and liquor left with which to entertain themselves. Nestor's response to my decision, was to begin screaming in loud, drunken indignation, "You can't refuse me. I am rich! I am a very rich man." He leapt up, trying to hold his tattered pants up with one hand, but they fell below his knees when he reached for a bottle of gin. "I'm rich! I'm rich! I'm rich!" he shouted, then turned and ran wildly out of the village without further explanation.

I had already taken some good photographs of the most important Ifugao ritual, and this seemed like a good time to leave, before the drunken fiasco got any further out of hand. It was starting to rain, and even if the party continued I would not be able to work in the downpour. I handed 500 pesos to Nestor's mother. I had agreed to pay the final 1,000 pesos if and when they completed all of the performances, but it was obvious that the intoxicated revelers were in no condition to continue. I wanted Nestor to be satisfied with our transaction, but I didn't want to be exploited and felt that half of the balance due should be enough to satisfy him. I returned to my hut, collected my

belongings, and began to hike back alone over the mountain to Batad Junction. By the time I reached the road it was dark, already exhausted I felt my legs buckling under me, but I was still emotionally charged from the day's events. I peered up and down the road and unwittingly set off in the wrong direction. It was unlikely I would find any transportation untill dawn, no matter how far I wandered. After about two miles, my legs finally gave out and I collapsed in a heap on the side of the road. In the distance, a glimmer of light flickered through the leaves and branches ahead. My hope renewed as I dragged myself back up to the road using a broken branch for a cane. I stumbled up onto the roadway, causing the skull Gem-o gave me to roll out of my pack and land upright in the path before me. This was an eerie sight indeed: a black skull staring at me hauntingly from the middle of a deserted road in the light of the full moon now rising behind a thick canopy of trees and hanging vines. This bizarre apparition frightened me so much I threw away my walking stick and raced unaided toward the light in the distance. The source turned out to be a "sari-sari," a mom and pop grocery store in the middle of nowhere. Out front, four men were silently playing cards under a lone flickering light bulb. I walked up and sat down at the table without a word. To my astonishment, they dealt another hand

The beginning of the "Mom batak" harvest ritual (above)
"Gem-o" offers the sacrificial pig (facing page)
The mountain leading to Batad Junction and the skull (top)

and accepted me into their game as if I were a neighbor they had been waiting for all night. Not wanting to appear ungrateful, I took a swig from a bottle of gin that was passed around the table and pretended to be wide awake. I really wanted a ride back to the security of Banaue, where food and shelter awaited me, but I knew that if I seemed too desperate I might never reach a safe haven.

When the gin bottle came around a second time, I proposed a bold wager— if I lost the next round, I would give them 200 pesos in exchange for a ride to Banaue, but if I won the hand they would give me a ride for free. They accepted my terms gleefully, thinking the offer far too generous, but I purposely lost the hand by discarding all my jacks to a player I suspected of collecting them, and folded my cards when he took the hand easily. I threw a 100 peso note on the table, acting as if I was bitterly disappointed. I would pay them the balance, I announced, if and when we got to Banaue. Within minutes they had procured a rickety old jeepney with baling wire and rope holding the dilapidated cab and truck bed to the chassis. I was overjoyed at the sight of the decrepit vehicle and scrambled into the back, but the amiable driver beckoned me to sit next to him in the forward passenger compartment. En route, we picked up additional paying passengers. The driver tempted even the

most unwilling wanderers with discounted fares. As the jeepney filled up, we all began singing aloud as I chewed greedily on some strong betel nuts produced by one of the delighted passengers. I lapsed into the trance-like state of a somnambulant daydream and continued my strange nocturnal journey in this happy daze. At some point I must have fallen asleep, since I have no recollection of arriving at my hotel or climbing into bed. I was awakened at dawn by loud banging on the door of my room at the People's Lodge. Nestor and two of his comrades stood in the doorway with a Banaue policeman, ordering him to arrest me for not paying the full amount owed for the ritual performances. Half an hour later, I found myself in a makeshift courtroom facing the arresting officer, now presiding as the town magistrate. As Nestor angrily accused me of cheating him, I remembered our contract and pulled the crumpled document from my back pocket.

"Gem-o" waving goodby
"Gem-o" and his hunting dog on the
mountains above Batad (facing page)

I handed it to the magistrate, explaining I had only received half of the stipulated services
and had already paid for a pig, three chickens, and three bottles of gin. The bemused judge read the
words slowly, then asked Nestor if the thumbprint on the agreement was indeed his. Now confident of
victory Nestor agreed it was his, and the policeman who had turned into a judge, thought for a moment
before reaching his verdict. The plaintiffs, he announced, would have to return all the money I had paid
them, since they had violated the contract by becoming inebriated in public, and failing to deliver the
required number of performances. Panicking at this unexpected reversal, Nestor and his two friends
bolted out of their seats and ran to the door, fleeing down the hallway and out of the little courthouse.
I walked to the window and watched in amusement as they raced past squealing pigs, clucking chickens
and startled vendors in the crowded marketplace. In their haste, they took a messy shortcut
through the town dump, then disappeared down an alleyway at the other end of

the town square, moving rapidly in the general direction of the trail back to their village of Batad. This dramatic exit seemed a fitting end to my adventures. It suddenly seemed the right moment to take my leave of the islands. I ran back to the People's Lodge, stuffed my bag full with cameras and artifacts, and tossed the room key on to the checkout counter on my way out. Within an hour I was on a bus heading back to Manila and the International Airport. As I gazed out a grimy window, I reflected on the incongruous mixture of primitive and complex emotions these mountain tribespeople had displayed. In a few short months, they had shown me more spontaneous, unfeigned generosity and authentic spirituality than I had encountered in an entire lifetime. On this journey I had discovered Paradise is a state of mind, rather than a place. I now look back on the tribes' paradoxical combination of compassion and aggression, creative innovation and stern traditionalism, knowing I have found a remedy for the spiritual void in my Western world.

TRIBES

Danee: The young boy from Tinglayan who probably stole the camera.

Daging: The Kalinga headhunter from the village of Poblacion.

Owong-Ayyag: The Kalinga headhunter's wife from Tinglayan.

Gem-o: The Ifugao shaman who hunted and served snake meat in Batad.

Yaing: The Kalinga woman with beautifully tattooed arms from the village of Luplupa.

Istak: One of the old Kalinga headhunters from Tinglayan.

PEOPLE

Malong: The Kalinga girl who gave a hat as a present in the village of Bot-Bot.

Lumatac: The receptive and friendly Kalinga headhunter from Tulgao.

Lingayon: The old Ifugao woman who sold artifacts in the town of Banaue.

Puyao: The Kalinga warrior from Ambato village who took seven heads.

Mongit: The Ifugao leader and shaman from the village of Tam-an.

Narciso: The Ifugao shaman who cured the sick by sacrificing chickens.

CONVERSATIONS
THREE KALINGA HEADHUNTERS

Lumatac

An elderly hunter-gatherer and farmer from the village of Tulgao, Lumatac lives with his wife in a small thatched hut. His four children have long since abandoned the Kalinga ways, adopting Christianity and migrating from the village. One of the last three surviving headhunters in Tulgao, he proudly bears the "fatoc" tattoo on his chest. His words are translated by a fellow Kalinga tribesman, Francis Pa-in.

D: What is your name and your village?
L: I am Lumatac from Tulgao.
D: When were you born?
L: I do not really know, there was no calendar in my village then.
D: How many heads have you taken?
L: Two.
D: Why did you go headhunting?
L: When the peace pact with Lubo was broken, that was when we went to get their heads!
D: How long ago was that?
L: A long time back, when I was a bachelor-- about twenty years ago.
D: Did you headhunt very many times?
L: No, only that one time to Lubo village. I took two heads then, and we did the big dance called "mamar" when we got home.
D: Did you have a special ritual before you went headhunting?
L: Yes. We listened for the sound of the birds, and when the sound was good we knew it was time to go headhunting. We called this "machongal," and the name of the bird is the "echaw."
D: How many headhunters were there when you were young?
L: About 30, I guess, but not all of them had the "fatoc" chest tattoo like I do. Only two came with me to take heads in Lubo that day. Most of them are dead now; there are only three left and I am one of them!
D: What do you remember best about the old headhunting days?
L: Well, I can tell you, if you become a headhunter the girls like you very much, because you are a hero. When I went on the raid, I was very frightened before the fighting began, but once the "faronit" (battle) started, I had no fear at all. Because they had broken the peace pact and killed our men, I knew it was right to kill the men from Lubo and take their heads.

Puyao

Puyao was born in Ambato village nearly a century ago. A prolific and experienced headhunter, Puyao proudly displayed jawbones from a few of his many victims, used as handles for his ritual gongs. He wore the "fatoc" tattoo indicating his status as a headhunter warrior.

D: What is your name? What village are you from?
P: I am Puyao, from Ambato Dalag.
D: Do you know how old you are?
P: I am 90 years.
D: Are you a Kalinga warrior?
P: Oh yes! I have taken seven heads!
D: Where did you take those heads? Was it at Kalinga villages? Did you fight the people of the Ifugao or Bontoc tribes?
P: No, I headhunted in Kalinga villages;--Tubuk, Lubuagan and Basao.
D: You gave me a gong handle made from a human jaw. Was that from one of your victims?
P: Yes, of course.

D: Do you still practice the old rituals today?

P: Yes, we still perform the "lalo," the dance that we do when we butcher a carabao or a pig just before we go headhunting.

D: When was the last time you took a head?

P: It was many years ago... 1943. During World War II I helped the American soldiers to gather supplies. When the Japanese came, I took many of their heads to help my people win the war.

D: Can you sing one of the old headhunting songs for me?

P: Yes, I know the "Song of the Warrior," that is the song we always sing before we go headhunting.

Daging

D: What is your name and your village?

DG: I am Daging from Poblacion village.

D: How old are you?

DG: I do not really know.

D: Well, how many heads have you taken?

DG: Five.

D: What villages did they come from?

DG: I did not headhunt in the villages, only outside the villages.

D: When did you last actually take a head?

DG: It was in the 1940s, I think.

D: Do you still perform the headhunting rituals?

DG: Yes, I do the "falos" headhunting ritual to remember the old days.

D: Do Kalinga headhunters have a special god?

DG: Yes, the name of the god is "Kabunian." Our religion does not have a special name, only the god "Kabunian." He tells us what is good and bad, and guides the people. When the harvest comes we do the "papitian" ritual for the rice and bring food to all the people.

D: Did headhunters from other villages ever come to attack you and your people?

DG: Yes, they came from Lubo to Tinglayan Poblacion, shouting at us and waving their spears. After the fight started we battled with them for more than one hour! We fought them with axes, spears, knives. When your people kill another people, what do you use to fight the enemy?

D: Well, I don't kill other people, but my country has many big guns and giant airplanes that can drop bombs from the skies.

DG: Have many people died from these planes and bombs you use to kill America's enemies?

D: I am afraid they have. There have been so many people killed by America's machines that I could not count them.

DG: Is your country in the center of the ocean?

D: No country is really in the center of the ocean, the world is round. My country is a part of this same world as yours.

DG: I would like to come to America to see if that is so!

D: You are certainly welcome to come whenever you can, but for now I can only bring back your picture and show the people in America what a Kalinga headhunter looks like.

DG: I will be happy for them to see me then!

THREE MOMBAKI SHAMANS

Narciso Riag

Narciso Riag is revered and honored by the villagers of Batad. He is one of the few Mombaki shamans still practicing the traditional Ifugao "Baki" rituals. When I first met him, he was conducting the "canao" ritual sacrifice with his fellow Mombaki shamans, in hopes of curing one of the ailing village elders.

D: I'm interested in what you're doing today. Are you making a sacrifice?

N: Yes, we were playing "canao" because there is a sick person in this house. It began with the old folks who taught us to do "canao." The priest brings the wine, the sacred bowl and the ceremonial box. You see, the priest is praying to his dead ancestors, asking them for help so that the sick person will soon be better. It is called an offering. We have no special prayer, it is just us asking with words spoken out loud. We say if you or other messengers are causing the sickness of this person, we are making this offering of a chicken to you.

D: How does the priest know if the ritual has worked?

N: They can look at the liver of the chicken. They give this special part to the priest, and he sees if the liver is good. After we sacrifice two or three chickens, if the livers all look the same, we believe the person might recover. But if the liver is bad, or if there is a difference in the three livers, then the priest might have to play another "canao." The priest will explain to the owner of the house that there is a problem about the liver, so they have to do something, perhaps sacrifice and offer a pig. We also perform this ritual when there is some problem in our family, and we are asking our god to help us. After asking for help in our own way, we stand in front of the ritual box and the bowl with wine. One person holds the feet of the chicken, and one person takes a special knife and kills the chicken. After that we can burn the feathers of the chicken, and when we see the liver we know if the spirits have accepted our offering of the chicken.

D: What is the name of your god?

N: "Macnoman" is what we call the god, and if Macnoman likes the offering, then the family will be okay and the offering is successful. So that is our medicine, because before there was your Western medicine, the Ifugao were always making these offerings to our dead ancestors. Macnoman is just asked for help in this way. And if we wake up in the night and hear a group of fireflies going up into heaven we will pray so the fireflies will come back down to earth. But if the fireflies keep going up, that means an Ifugao person will die because Macnoman has not accepted the sacrifice. And now the younger generation, they are praying to another god in the church, but we compare the younger generation's ways to our old ways of the village without shame.

Mongit

Mongit is an elder of the Ifugao tribe from the village of Tam-an. His words reveal an intense awareness of the living presence of his ancestors' spirits. Mongit speaks the dialect of Banaue, and his words are translated by Robin Comple, a student of the Beyers, a family of German anthropologists who founded the Ifugao Museum in Banaue.

D: What is that wooden box you use in your rituals?

M: "Punam han" is what we call this box. We use it to put our sacrifice in when we do our "Baki" rituals. That is what our forefathers did a long time ago.

D: Why do you perform your "Baki" rituals with this box?

M: You can learn if you have sickness, you can do this prayer and get rid of the sickness. The prayer cures sickness. Not everybody still believes in it.

M: Inside the ceremonial box we put one, two or maybe three betel nuts, and pieces of rice from the field. Part of a sacrificed chicken is mixed with the nuts and rice as an offering to god.

D: How long do the rituals last?

M: An important ritual like the harvest ritual begins at seven o'clock in the evening and it will last almost two days with no sleep. A healing ritual like "canao" will only last until about noon, so it would last five hours-- about half a day.

D: Are these rituals still the most important part of the Ifugao religion?

M: Not for everyone. But the ceremony is still important to many of us, and it has to be done right. We pour blood over the "bulul" rice god. Once a year we give drinks to the "bulul" rice guardian. We put wine on the head of the "bulul" to make all the wine turn out good. These rituals are important to me, and many other Ifugao people also believe they are important and useful.

Gem-o Mang-hi

Gem-o, a "Mombaki" shaman, proved to be more familiar than most with the particulars of the various healing, harvest and fermentation rituals. He was concerned that his people's encounter with modern civilization and technology would cause their culture to disintegrate. Like Narciso, he wanted to be sure his contacts with foreigners alerted them to the endangered status of the Ifugao people and culture. He is a friend of Narciso and like his friend is a Mombaki shaman from the village of Batad. His words are translated by a fellow Ifugao tribesman, Bernabe Mamanglo.

Q: What is the name of your Ifugao religion and why do you believe in it?

G: "Baki" is the name of our religion. I follow it because it can be used to cure sickness and to see into the future.

Q: Please tell me how you perform "Baki."

G: Usually "Baki" is performed using many things, like the ritual box, bowls and sometimes the bulul rice guardians. With sacrifices and chanting, we call our dead ancestors' spirits to join our group and help with our needs.

Q: Are all the rituals called "Baki"?

G: Yes, but in "Baki" there are many types of sacrifices and performances for birth, marriage, sickness, death; all important events in the Ifugao life are celebrated in "Baki." During the rituals we also dance. We call the dance "bayo." We dance while we play a gong in many of our rituals. We also have a ritual when the rice is being harvested we call "Mom-batak." Only once a year at the harvest they bring out the "Bulul" rice guardian. We always keep this statue in the granary. During the ritual, they bring out the ceremonial box with the bulul statue. Then a chicken or pig is killed and we put the animals blood on the box and the "bulul" figure. It brings back the spirit and brings the "bulul" to life.

Q: How many priests participate in this ritual?

G: Some rituals need five to ten. When there are sick persons, they use many priests.

Q: Do you think your religion will continue to survive? Narciso said the young people are becoming Christians.

G: I really feel that something should be done to protect this culture, because all these rituals are my heritage. The Christians say that this is pagan. But actually not all the rituals are pagan. Some of the rituals compare to the rituals in Christianity. Something should be done to help preserve the old Ifugao traditions and rituals. I hope they will be saved...

Peter Gothic: AN IFUGAO TRIBESMAN

Peter Gothic was one of the most articulate and well traveled of all the native people I encountered during this journey. Although born into the Ifugao tribe during the days when headhunting was still practiced, he later learned to read and write. On reaching adulthood, Peter took up a career as a guide and interpreter for Western visitors. He has worked with many foreigners: a social scientist from Denmark, an English photojournalist, and a French anthropologist with whom he went on a one-year artifact collecting expedition among the Ifugao in 1986.

Q: Please tell me about yourself and the Ifugao people...

P: If the old ways are lost, it will be like the setting of the sun. Life is like the rising and the setting of the sun. When the sun rises an empire or a kingdom is born, and when the sun sets the kingdom or empire will die so that another can be born. But in the Ifugao tradition, we have another way: "Daya" is the bringer of life and death, and all will come from "Daya." "Daya" will bring all things together, and this is like the setting and the rising of the sun as one. I will die one day. Then these stories I tell will only be in the ground. But now I will say, Feel your soul so you know the soul. Feel the river so you know the river and feel the soul of the river so you will know your own soul's river.

TRIBAL RELIGION

SACRED RITUALS
OF THE MOUNTAIN TRIBES

The Ifugao were designated as the "Igorots" by the conquering Spaniards in the 18th century, and it was the Ifugao people who made the most "deliberate and successful resistance to Spanish settlement in their territory." For the ardently Catholic Spaniards, the pagan Ifugao religion was deeply repugnant, and eradication of their traditional native religion became a priority of the soldiers and missionaries. Fortunately, the core elements of the Ifugao beliefs have been preserved. The Ifugao religion, known as "Baki," is an elaborate set of rituals, practices and beliefs centered around a pantheistic belief in the forces of the natural world. Baki shamanism is the most advanced form of all the mountain tribal religions, having been nurtured and developed over many centuries in concert with a sophisticated artistic tradition. The Ifugao's belief structure is a combination of medicine, art and tribal law. Although pagan in form and practice, Baki has many conceptual parallels with Christianity, from the central role of the icons or wooden idols to the ritual sacrifice of body and blood in the main liturgies. In both religions, a force embodying the ultimate power is invoked through the intermediary figure of a sculpted human form.

The pantheon of Ifugao deities is small but complex, being divided roughly into "pili" or protective gods (of which the rice guardian "bulul" is the most important) and "hipag" or war gods. These figures are represented by small or middle-sized carved wooden figures with essentially human forms, kept in small shrines or special storage areas near the property being protected and only invoked through a particular ritual or sacrifice on behalf of the god. The "bulul," similar in form and function to the Bontoc and Kankanay "anito" and "tinanatago", is a rice guardian which is kept in the granary year-round and brought out on the occasion of the special sacrificial "Mom batak" ritual, which is performed during the rice harvest. The "hipag" figures, on the other hand, may be in the form of animals such as roosters, ducks, or wild boars, as well as human beings. Here the carved figures have considerably less influence as idols and objects of veneration, and are rather used to call the god to assist the owner in the event of some personal conflict or in times of impending warfare. The figure is typically smeared with sacrificial animal blood, preferably of the type of the creature represented by the figure, at which time the figure assumes extraordinary power. The "hipag" figurines are usually smaller and less elaborately carved than the "bulul" figures, but they too are stored in baskets or protective places and only brought out when needed; the deity is thus not omnipresent, but only activated through special Baki rituals.

There are "Baki" rituals for all the needs of Ifugao life-curing and healing, fermentation of the rice wine, blessing the rice harvest, or any purpose deemed fit by the "Mombaki" Ifugao priest. Many of the rituals involve the use of a wooden ceremonial box or "punam han", which is the pagan equivalent of the Christian tabernacle. In this box are placed the sacrificial blood, betel nuts, bones and feathers, or scraps of pig, chicken meat, and occasionally a "hipag," all deposited together in an offering to the supreme god of the Ifugao people. The "hipag" rituals are not associated with any special events, on the other hand, but are invoked in matters involving personal conflicts, mortal offense or the need for revenge on one's enemies. The appropriate carved wooden figure are carefully stored in the "punam han" offertory box, which can be owned by anyone wealthy enough to afford to have one carved to order. In the event the individual is too poor, however, the rituals can still be performed without the ceremonial box.

The sacrifice of a pig or chicken is a central feature of many Ifugao rituals; it helps to stave off the celebrants' hunger during the long ceremony that follows, a ceremony which may last anywhere from five hours at the shortest to over thirty-six hours at the longest. The "Mom batak" harvest sacrifice of the pig is a major tribal event and the most important Ifugao ritual. The animal's blood is placed on the body of the wooden "bulul" idol and poured over the exterior of the "punam han" ritual box, in the belief that its vital strength will enhance the sacrifice and bring the "bulul" back to life with renewed energy when consecrated with the sacrificial blood. The sacrifice summons the tribal ancestors by using the "bulul" as a medium or channel to reach the god, whose blessing will insure a successful rice harvest. The importance of the "bulul" figures can e judged by the fact that they are inherited by the first born along with the rice fields and ranaries they protect.

The artifacts employed in the harvest ritual consist of carved wooden rice guardians or bululs," a ceremonial box, plates, spoons, and rice wine cups. The wooden "bulul" figures, usually ne male and one female, are placed on either side of the "punam han" ceremonial box during he rice ritual. Sacrificial elements of animal blood, bones, feathers and other items are placed in he box between the two figures. Primitive bamboo percussion instruments are sounded, etitioning the god in hopes of achieving a successful harvest and safe storage of the rice.

The deep spell of the ritual lasts many hours, as the priests chant and play their gongs to rown out the cries of the animals being slaughtered. The priests chant in unison, then in call and esponse, finally reaching a trance state similar to that attained by Buddhist priests through neditation or chanting of mantras.

Upon completion of the sacrifice, the villagers return to their daily routine. Once the harvest completed and the rice is placed in the granary, the bululs also are returned to the granary to id in the ongoing protection of the rice. It should be remembered the "bulul" is in fact not a god, ut only a rice guardian figure which acts as a spiritual conduit to the supreme Ifugao god. This antheistic figure is cited by many anthropologists and religious authorities as evidence of a trong monotheistic bent to Ifugao religion. The rice guardians are the property of the owner of the ranary, typically one of the wealthiest landowners in the village, who assumes the responsibility or all the expenses and preparations for the harvest ritual. Each village has several large andowners with private granaries, containing several "bululs" or pairs of "bulul" figures. Other illagers may possess their own "bulul" idols and use them without the aid of a priest, but the rincipal traditional village rituals must be performed by acknowledged Ifugao shamans. The naman traditionally possesses the sacrificial "punam-han" ceremonial box, but must get the oulul" idols from the landowner as well as his permission for their use. There is considerable ompetition for the privilege of paying for the public ceremonies of feasting and dancing, which equire large amounts of food and drink to be supplied to the entire village. When an Ifugao cquires sufficient wealth and status to be a "kadangyan" or noble, it is expected he will sponsor ne public ceremony, organize the festivities and pay for the appropriate sacrifices. Afterward, this

Ifugao ceremonial spoons with bulul figure handles

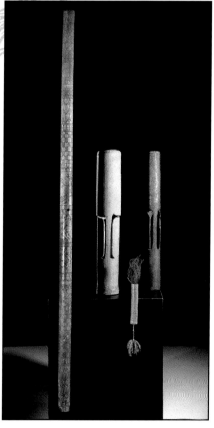

Kalinga nose flute, Ifugao bamboo percussion instruments, and Kalinga bamboo mouth harp

(above): Four Ifugao architectural "bulul" figures used as: house posts, door frames, and hearth shelving

(below): The Ifugao "higabi" wooden bench is a privileged status symbol of wealth
(The Field Museum collection # 22273)

individual will be eligible to own the "hagabi" wooden bench which is the principal Ifugao symbol of wealth and privilege. The "hagabi" itself, which is proudly displayed in front of the owner's house for all the village to see, often requires considerable effort in searching for the right wood, supplying the woodcarvers with food and drink, and carving the trunk. The large bench is then transported back to the house of the new owner, who sponsors another three days of festivities in celebration of his arrival into the Ifugao upper class.

The "Dyato" ritual is performed during the preparation of "tapuy," the strong local wine made from rice. The purpose of this variant of the harvest ritual is to speed the fermentation of wine. In this ritual a single standing "bulul" rather than a pair of seated wooden figures is usually employed. The standing figure's head has either an open skull cavity or a cup-shaped depression carved directly into its crown, which becomes the receptacle used for the consecration of the wine. When pouring the liquid into the head, it is hoped the wine will drain all the way down through the figure to emerge from the feet by penetrating through the entire body of the idol. If the wine successfully negotiates the prescribed path through the figure, a successful fermentation of the rice is foretold. The tribes therefore go to great lengths to make sure the wine passes through the idol properly, with the celebrants in some cases becoming fixated as they attempt to assist the miraculous passage of the wine through the body of the standing figure.

The ceremonial standing or seated bulul figures are reserved for the most important "Baki" rituals. However, the bulul is incorporated into everyday life by means of architecture. Ifugao house posts, doors and hearth shelves are frequently decorated with carvings in the form of a bulul.

The Ifugao's healing ritual; "Canao", uses one or more chickens and a wooden "punam han" offertory box, but no bulul figures. Gathering on the ground in front of the hut during "Canao", the "Mom-Baki" shamans visit and talk with the ailing inhabitant. After chanting and sacrificing the first chicken, the liver's color is examined by the shamans, who divine from it the eventual recovery or demise of the sick individual. A sacrifice of up to three chickens may be performed if the first finding is deemed questionable, and if this fails to produce the desired results, a pig may be a required sacrifice.

Each of the three main rituals has its own special designation. "Mom batak" is the harvest ritual, where "bulul" pairs from the granary are usually brought out with a ceremonial box, the "Canao" healing ritual is always practiced with the offertory box, and frequently with vessels and plates, but no "bulul" and the "Dyato" rice wine fermentation ritual usually employs a single "bulul" idol, while ceremonial drinking is done from star-shaped, triangular or circular bowls or cups.

All these rituals are performed regularly throughout the Ifugao Province even today. The immediate objectives of these three Ifugao rituals are practical rather than self consciously spiritual: to heal, to speed the fermentation of the wine, and to insure the success of the rice harvest. The ultimate purpose of these sacrifices, however, is the spiritual reintegration of the villagers with their gods and ancestors, whose continuing presence is so vital to the life of the Ifugao people.

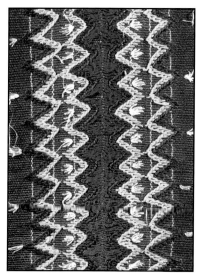
Kalinga tribal colors

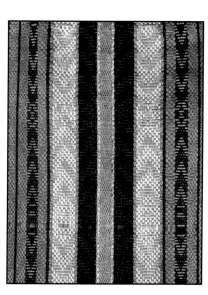
Ifugao tribal colors

Bontoc tribal colors

TRIBAL LAW
WAR AND PEACE
AMONG THE MOUNTAIN TRIBES

While the Ifugao people are perhaps the best representatives of the artistic and religious culture of the highlands, the Kalinga are paradoxically the best exemplars of the region's tribal custom law. The Kalinga have long been rightly regarded as the most aggressive and warlike of the highlands tribespeople and their pacification represented the greatest challenge to the Spanish and American colonialists. The legal suppression of headhunting was only achieved after three centuries of active conflict among the various tribes and the forces of civilization, which penetrated the surrounding lowlands early in the 16th century, and only during the 20th century brought the highlands under complete control.

The formidable reputation of the warlike Kalinga is perhaps misleading in some respects, for they inhabit some of the best crop lands in the Cordillera, and were the last to come to rice paddy cultivation methods because of the abundant local resources for hunting and gathering. "Not only are the Kalingas better supplied with food than the other tribes-they are better housed... The Kalinga house is an admirable one, and the Kalinga woman keeps it well..." (R.F.Barton, 1949:9-10). In some other respects, Kalinga tribal custom is esoteric and unique; for example, "the priesthood is almost entirely in the hands of women" who enter it as a calling taught by older priestesses, although today most ritual sacrifice is conducted by male tribal leaders. Nevertheless, the Kalinga reputation for pugnacity is legitimate.

The key institution in the pacification of the Kalinga and the other mountain tribes was the peace pact, an ancient tribal tradition which was used by the Spanish and the Americans to expand individual village pacts and treaties into a broader regional framework. Today, hundreds of peace pacts exist between the various villages, areas and tribes, both within an individual Province, like Kalinga, and between divergent Provinces. These peace pacts represent the single strongest legal and judicial influence in a region where the authority of the Filipino federal government is still limited.

The origins of the peace pact are obscure and some researchers go so far as to assert that peace pacts are a tradition dating back to before the first colonial intrusion, even to prehistoric times. It stands to reason that neighboring villages and tribes could not maintain a state of perpetual warfare. In a system based on honor and revenge, it only makes sense that some normative basis-- a state of peace the violation of which required equivalent retaliation or retribution-- should be defined. Still, there is no evidence that any formal peace pact existed before the advent of civilization and the European influence, and it seems clear that the explicit peace pact is a foreign institution, one that has been used mainly to quell conflicts among the rebellious natives over the last century.

In its original indigenous form, the peace pact was a device whereby neighboring villages and precincts or "barangays" could agree to remain at arm's length, especially among the Kalinga who typically fought and raided on a seasonal basis. The typical offenses that required a headtaking expedition were either murder or theft, but more nebulous feuds were carried on for decades and the urge to kill was considered a natural and instinctive part of the warrior's life. According to different observers, the most common source of tribal enmity was invariably theft of livestock, adultery, illicit unions, or assault.

Whatever priority these offenses take today, however, most authorities on highlands tribal law agree that the only peace pacts before the 20th century were local and provisional in character. The Kalinga in particular were in need of a more formal peace institution, as their territory had (and still has) at least 55 recognizable divisions. In recognition of this need, the American authorities went to great pains to encourage the formalization and extension of the peace pact system to the entire province. Kalinga tribal law constitutes an oral tradition, and it is a misnomer to speak of legal codes or judicial proceedings, except in connection with the superimposition of the Filipino government's legal system.

However, the essential core of tribal law (as distinct from tribal custom) is contained in a well-defined oral contract known as the peace pact or "badong." This pact covers a wide-range

Batad

Cambulo

Cambulo

Cambulo

Tulgao

Bot bot

of offenses, and although it is primarily directed at conflicts between villages and tribes, it also contains the nucleus of tribal law concerning crimes of violence, property rights, and other matters ranging from adultery to slander. It should be noted from the outset that under Filipino law, headhunting has long been illegal, and thus the tribal peace pacts never speak directly of the consequences when the pact is broken. As the most ritualized form of tribal conflict even headhunting had its own limited set of rules and legal procedures; no warrior would violate these rules lest he become an outcast among his own people. Still, the headhunting ritual was basically a legal interim during which all normal rules and standards of fair play were temporarily suspended, including any notions of self-sacrifice or pretense of direct retaliation against the offending party. In this regard, the Kalinga share the attitude of most primitive peoples toward raiding: "...attacks are made only when some advantage will accrue to the attacker. Ambushes of various sorts are devised. At such times no distinction is made between the able-bodied members of the tribe and the children or the old people. A head is a head, regardless." (Krieger, 1942: 71)

In short, the peace pact governs the normal operations of Kalinga society in peacetime, while in times of war a spirit of anarchy prevails. Ritual and form are followed with great precision, but without strict limits on the violent excesses of active combat. A remarkable document, "The Making of Kalinga Pagta/Bodoonog," written by the Kalinga tribesman,

Francis Pain, presents some of the best direct evidence of the traditional and symbolic character of the peace pact. Pain maintains that the Kalingas had their own laws for the "ili" or village long before the arrival of any Western influence, and that the "pagta" (pact) or "bodong" (peace agreement) was introduced only to formalize the rules on a regional basis. Indeed, according to Francis Pain, the very name "Kalinga," means warrior, and it was the warning cry of the neighboring villagers when a raiding party was heading their way, telling them to "run away or to hide so that they may not kill or capture them" to keep as slaves.

Francis Pain has transcribed and translated the "Basao-Tinglayan Peace Pact," an unwritten treaty between the "ili" or villages of Basao and Luplupa, near Tinglayan in Kalinga-Apayao Province (just recently divided into separate districts by the Filipino national government). The preamble of this "supreme law" of the Kalinga describes its purpose as to "promote peace in solving our village problems, after our sorrows experienced in the past village conflict" and to "have a better and more lasting friendship, strictly guarded by all the village inhabitants as eyes, ears, arms, and feet, putting into the peace pact holder the burden of honor and responsibility." (Pain, 1994)

The body of the treaty opens with a description of the specific territories covered by the agreement and a declaration of the parties and peoples covered by the pact. Pain notes that tribal members are covered regardless of their physical location. The list of crimes, offenses and slights covered by the pact is extensive, and each violation is ascribed a particular penalty. To begin with, "crimes against persons" include first and foremost the killing of any inhabitant of the two villages party to the pact, in which case "the pagta shall be broken" at once.

Serious physical injuries that fall short of murder are equally a violation of the pact, however, recognizing the principle of intent as critical to the interpretation of the crime. There is, however, no distinction made between "killing" (as in causing the accidental death of someone) and murder as such.

The list of secondary offenses covered by the pact describes any crimes which do break the peace pact. These include offenses against honor, such as libel against a woman's character, to be compensated by the payment of a carabao cow to the victim; breach of contract, to be punished by a "sanction" against the debtor to be paid to the injured party; and stealing, where for example the theft of a carabao cow is to be punished by a double payment, one carabao for the owner/victim, and one carabao for his village. As it is presumed the carabao is killed and consumed quickly to conceal the crime, the perpetrator is not expected to return the stolen animal itself.

On the other hand, the second required animal offered as punitive damage retribution is "butchered and distributed equally to the houses of the umili," or injured party's village, as a gesture of public humiliation requiring the thief to perform the slaughter and sacrifice an additional time. An entirely separate category of crimes and punishments is described for violations concerning land, including unlawful use for a residence, rice cultivation, pasture, vegetable gardening, or even hunting. Kalinga law is surprisingly explicit with regard to land tenure, acquisition, and classification perhaps because no formal documentation or land title is required by traditional tribal law. The pact covers the forest and pasture lands of the tribal commons, family clan, and communal fishing rights, as well as, private land. These land boundaries are fixed at the original "ili bugis" or village borders, "except additional new land acquired', which set the limits by an outer perimeter.

Another such peace pact, between Tinglayan and Madocayong, is more explicitly a territorial agreement, and takes the form of a written legal document signed by a prominent leader of each community. This contract basically reiterates the crimes and their consequences as found in the previous pact, but constitutes an even more formal arrangement for payment of compensation or "utang" to the injured party or parties.

All peace pacts naturally require agreement and formal acceptance before they gain the force of a legal contract. As Francis Pain translates the procedural rules, the assumption is that the tribal peace has already been broken, and that the pact is only restored when both sides "want peace again." When this occurs, one member of the tribe is chosen by the elders to send his machete or spear to the other tribe; if the weapon is peacefully received by the representatives of that tribe, then the peace pact is made or restored. There follows an "inom," or discussion of the past conflict and the nature of the new peace, in an "oratory form of debate" which would do credit to western lawmakers and litigants. In a "proper inom" all the young men are made to listen to this debate, after which a gong is sounded and a celebration ensues "where the gentlemen and ladies of the two tribes share their enjoyment" of a butchered carabao cow or pig, and exchange gifts of various sorts.

The maintenance of any peace pact covering a wide range of offenses between any and all members of two villages or tribes is a tenuous proposition. The Kalinga prescribe a number of rituals and festivities to overcome any residual hard feelings, including a "funong" or "warm visitation" of groups from one tribe to another, a "fogga" or mourning party sent to visit in the event of an illness or death among the other tribe, and numerous other formal payments of tribute, respect or compensation.

Blood relations are bound by the pact and by higher forms of obligation as well. If there is extended kinship between the villages, relatives may invite distant family members to visit and feast with them to strengthen their bond. Significantly, the Kalinga peace pact is considered to be hereditary in nature, and its acceptance is transferred from parent to child, renewing the existing arrangement, even after the leaders who instigated the reigning peace agreement have died.

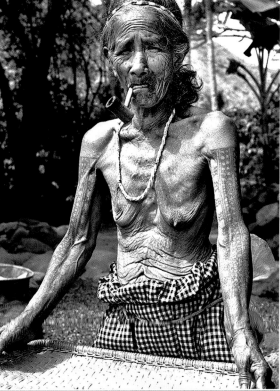

Kalinga female smoking "fang-fanga" pipe
Kalinga warriors "o-kong" hat.
Headhunting "pinagas" ax:
(The Field Museum # 18556),
Kalinga family gathered around the hearth:
(Eduardo Masferre 1950:
David Howard's collection)

CONCLUSION
UNITY OF ART
RELIGION AND MEDICINE

The hallmark of any intact primitive religion is continuity and unity in the central social funtions of healing, medicine and art. In the villages, literally every aspect of daily life is treated as a creative, aesthetic undertaking, in which art is of necessity a way of life. "Art" is not restricted to the making of artifacts, but extends to group activities, village politics, ritual ceremonies, hunting, cultivation, and all the innate proclivities of the tribe. The native artist creates an object, but the work is completely realized by a spiritual leader who uses the sculptural object as the centerpiece during the performance of sacred rituals.

The rejection of the Western notion of the "uncivilized" has a parallel in the world of art, which can be seen in the profound aesthetic and spiritual unity of what the West refers to as "primitive art", from sculpture, textiles and jewelry, to utilitarian objects. Creativity, nor art, are isolated from the totality of pure tribal life, and neither are treated as purely aesthetic or economic activities undertaken for their own sake.

The creativity is applied to virtually every activity of tribal life. Art and ritual, birth and death, war and peace-- all are finally one process. The unity of art, religion and medicine within a sacred object is not unique to the these tribes The belief in the spiritual power embodied in a symbolic object can be found among peoples living in all parts of the world and in every culture. The value of a sacred thing, whether a crucifix, a holy book, a great mosque or a cathedral, always comes from a instinctual mutual reference, and its power cannot be understood or felt without an open, receptive spirit. In this sense, the greatest work of an individual artist cannot approximate the power and value of a sacred piece of tribal art, which literally brings hope, healing and unity to the multi-leveled strata within village communities.

In many respects, the Western concept of a masterpiece of art is the product of a more narrow, compartmentalized vision than, for example, the Ifugao "bulul" statue, which incorporates within its form the knowledge, tradition and power of a people's religion, medicine and art. Any masterpiece created by a celebrated genius within the confines of the fine arts cultivated in the West is generally the expression of an egocentric, materialistic, object-oriented culture. The artwork is a "product", that has only non-functional aesthetic value. Where the work of fine art is isolated, sequestered in a museum or private collection, and studied in relation to competing works of greater or lesser popularity and price tags. The "bulul" , on the other hand, belongs immediately and eternally to the tribe and its gods. Hence it is rarely attributed to an individual artist or admired for its aesthetic merits alone.

Within the village, every man, woman and child is part of the extended tribal family community. But in a larger sense, belong to the even greater collective cosmos of tribes, who share a similar material existence and environment. The past, present and future, of these groups, are combined into a timeless non-linear spirit world. Life and death are a seamless continuum without beginning or end. Archetypal experience preceding one's personal existence merge into the present, coalescing into future and after-death experiences that are seen simultaneously and clairvoyantly.

This timeless element is lacking in Western empirical science, effectively preventing our total apprehension of the Universe. For the primitive, time is a non-linear continuum rather than a sharply defined compartmentalized framework, freeing one's mind to travel through the realm of instinct.

In this sense, religion, art and medicine are as essential and integral to the life of the tribal culture as are the material means of sustenance and physical survival. The tribal rituals and beliefs are indigenous in character and unique in their simplicity (remembering, of course, that the primitive is also, as Levi-Strauss reminds us, complex and highly-ordered).

For the outside observer, head-taking cannot be considered apart from the accompanying practices of shamanism, music, folk dance and art that are the vital center of the culture. Unlike in Western societies, ritual and daily life are woven into a seamless fabric. We must consider the headhunting ritual in the context of this larger culture of healing and medicine. The headhunting expedition, and its corollary the tribal peace pact, constitute the essential means of healing a wound in the body politic, the offense or pollution that requires a dramatic, violent but perfectly logical resolution in human blood. But the tribespeople's concept of healing medicine goes far beyond the taking of heads, to include a wide array of acts of atonement centered around the sacred artifacts-the ceremonial sacrificial box, the "bulul" figure, and the rites of animal sacrifice. To a surprising extent the tribes still treat healing as a function of ritual, although Western medicine has made its way into the larger towns and capital cities of the provinces. Traditional primitive medicine is a wisdom handed down, not through doctors or even midwives, but through the priests, whose role combines religion with medicine. The priest presides over the act of healing as a doctor, shaman, artist and minister to the afflicted.

The tribes share an all-pervasive belief in the magical quality of life and death; illness is usually not considered a medical phenomena, but rather an affliction caused by a pollution or by negative energies emerging from the spirit world. Such illnesses are best avoided through the careful observation of the purification rituals, rather than through any kind of preventive medicine or hygiene.

The traditional shaman considers medical treatment as an integral part of a religious ritual, rather than as a separate study and practice. The same forces cause sickness and epidemic diseases as cause other forms of bad luck or communal disaster like floods, and the same type of preventive rituals are used to counteract their influence. Purification is required after any contact with the unclean: death, physical deformity, insanity, sexual perversion, are all dangerously unclean. Illness is brought about by a failure to maintain the essential respectful connection to the gods and the forces of nature they control. Thus the priest comes to the house of the afflicted to make the necessary sacrifice, as much for the sake of the village as for the sake of the sick person. The ritual sacrifice appeases the gods, removes the curse, and restores the health of the community as a whole.

Since the mountain culture regards the healing arts as integrated aspects of religious ritual and daily life, the steps taken to protect the individual from illness essentially begin at birth, or even during pregnancy. The procreative act is recognized as the beginning of life. Just as other illnesses are treated as impurities, childbirth and its complications are also treated as occasions for renewed purification rituals and offerings.

Some anthropologists have observed the basic tribal concept of well-being and vitality to be based on a ritual use of sacrifice, music and dance to instill harmony in the body, beginning from childhood. From infancy to old age, life is perceived as a process of growth and spiritual development in which the body grows and decays in keeping with the overriding harmony of a natural cycle. The metaphor of life and growth as a ritual dance is not a purely poetic one, since the village children are taught dance movements from infancy in a creative process instilling rhythmic grace and ritual gestures at an early age.

At its highest state of transcendence, the concept of well-being merges into a kind of religious ecstasy exemplified in the trances and paranormal states of the priests and the celebrants. In this form of possession, the subject enters into a deep hypnotic state. The trance state is a learned faculty, signifying the presence of a particular god or demon, and is a gift that is admired and widely practiced even among young children.

Western skepticism about the efficacy of primitive medicine and healing rituals is based on a misunderstanding of the unified, cohesive world order of these peoples. What we call "medicine" is enlarged by the tribes into an entirely different spiritual and artistic dimension. There exists among the tribespeople an unbroken chain of rituals for purification, sacrifice and healing from birth to death, and at any given moment a similar link exists between folklore, the shaman's teachings and rituals, and the vital functions of daily life (which include art, music and dance in all aspects). Any application of modern Western medicine that takes place is treated as something apart from the ritual practices of healing, which not only help prevent sickness, but more significantly, facilitate and consecrate every aspect of life and growth, from birth to puberty, procreation and ultimately death.

For the Cordillera tribespeople of the Philippines, life and death are a continuous and fully integrated process of ritualized, symbolic display in which they give outward expression to the inner meaning and design of their ancient culture. The visible patterns of the culture are worn proudly and exhibited in numerous manifestations; as personal adornment in the form of tattoos, scarification and body painting, as tribal emblems found on clothing, musical instruments, headdresses; and in implements of war and peace. There is no suggestion of disguise, no element of subtlety, nor any attempt at deception or seduction; what is seen, touched, and heard is quite literally the soul and substance of the culture. Throughout the variety of cultural artifacts and designs of the tribes, a simple and consistent poetic correspondence is found.

The richness of a culture is a relative matter. The people of the Cordillera have certainly never experienced material affluence in the Western sense of the word. Their social and political economy operates completely without typical Western mechanisms of cultural exchange, such as the use of paper currency, the display of conspicuous consumption, and the universal coveting of other people's goods. Instead, the focus of tribal values is entirely on social and moral relations. Generosity and openness to strangers, compassion for all the people of the community, and a fierce sense of honor and personal integrity are universal traits of these people. The sharp contrast between the higher moral integrity of the headhunter tribes of the Cordillera Mountains as opposed to the Western-style corruption of the technologically advanced modern world is both paradoxical and ironic.

This profound cultural integrity goes beyond mere manners and instruments of exchange, to incorporate virtually every form of social and personal experience between birth and death. To the casual Western observer, accustomed to specialization, isolation and fragmentation of the social experience, the unity and fluidity of tribal life comes as a continual revelation. Where Westerners project personal distance and abstraction through such basic relations as material exchanges, social status and hierarchies of power, these simple tribespeople engage each other immediately, through gifts and rewards, constant displays of concern and affection, and collective as well as individual conceptions of well-being, happiness and abundance.

At the level of material production, these values are found in virtually every artifact handmade by these headhunting tribes, from the simplest tools for everyday use to the most extraordinary sacred ritual objects. Mass production and uniform patterns are unknown, for each work of art is an utterly unique creation by an individual artist-- and here everyone is an artist. The result is a society in which every person achieves a highly individualized and unique identity, as opposed to the spurious and strangely uniform displays of individualism found in the West.

The narrow Western concept of civilization implies a complicated social and religious order, legislated standards of morality, and serious concern for the rights and needs of all the members of society. Yet the reality of our advanced civilization is quite different-crass materialism, rampant racism, and a callous disregard for the beliefs and values of others abound in nearly every modern society. In light of this unpleasant reality, the simpler but more profound values of these tribespeople may well serve as a model for our own debased civilization.

The cultural contradiction between the complex and the primitive worlds would be little more than a cause for passing regret, were it not for the impending demise of this admirable culture. With the destruction of the last tangible evidence of the earliest human condition, our civilization will have lost touch with its own material and spiritual origins. In many respects, these proud but innocent people represent our better selves; the inner core of our essential human nature, where the sacred and the profane are intermingled and integrated most completely. With these peoples' disappearance, our own culture will have far fewer spiritual resources with which to redeem itself...

In a tropical climate where walls and doors are quite unnecessary, the indigenous architectural style of dwellings and public spaces is open and free-flowing. Each house is constructed of materials gathered locally by the inhabitants; the common living area in the hut is undivided. But where Westerners might feel a loss of their privacy and individual rights, these people feel only the absence of fear and selfishness. The interior space of the individual structure flows naturally into its neighbors' space, and the whole group of structures is a single organic entity-the village.

The typical domicile reflects the constant quest for the basic necessities of life: cooking and eating, sleep and shelter, work and play. Western obsessions with opulence, grandeur and eccentric individuality would not just be out of place here-they would be regarded as anti-social, even pathological. Instead, the profoundly socialized outlook of the tribe is manifested at every level. The need for proximity to others, for physicality in everyday social contact, and for mutual reassurance and security within the group, is felt everywhere. Food and shelter, goods and services-- all are offered freely and instinctively to neighbors and strangers alike. Even when food is scarce, it is always shared equally; to speak, sleep or work apart from others is unthinkable. The comfortable physical environment of the highlands-the warm tropical climate, abundance of natural resources, and tranquillity of village life-all encourage this idyllic state of affairs. The emotional and spiritual gratifications of the primitive world draw the villagers into a collective dream state, one that is entered freely and experienced deeply until the dreamer awakens...

In a land where nature, human beings and culture combine to create such a benevolent, nurturing reality, even the basic means of sustenance have been elevated to a high art. Foremost among these art forms are the rice terraces, the product of thousands of years of continuous and oving labor. Painstakingly dug out of the hillsides and constantly reinforced with thousands of stones, the rice terraces are suspended above the landscape like rivers in the sky.

The tribespeople themselves have little awareness or conscious appreciation of the aesthetic value of these structures, and regard them as a utilitarian means of subsistence. However, the conceptual and aesthetic genesis of these giant earthen forms is really more akin to that of the Egyptian pyramids, the Great Wall of China, and contemporary Western Environmental Art. While the original purpose of the rice terraces was purely functional, their enormous scale and intriguing patterns have given them the impact of a transcendental force of nature. Stone by stone, season by season, generation after generation, the rice terraces have been excavated, filled and shored up once again for continual reuse by future generations.

Today, we can see the end product of this endless struggle to master the physical landscape, a colossal airborne network of elevated ponds and streams, transforming the hills into a great mosaic synthesis of natural and man made elements. Building literally upon the foundation plans of their ancestors, the tribes continuously recreate the physical expression of their humanity in the mountains around them. The terraces thus extend the material and spiritual life of the tribe beyond the present, carrying the living past forever forward...

The attitude of the mountain tribespeople toward their deceased is indicative of their deep reverence for life. In provocative and sometimes comical ways, the living pay homage to the dead by having them reassume the roles and postures of life. Unlike the typical Western funeral, the tribal wake is viewed as a joyous final opportunity to share the company of the departed. The attitude and position of the corpse, seated upright in a chair, is a mark of the highest respect. The surviving members of the tribe gather around the deceased in their own chairs. The atmosphere is jubilant, and food and drink are served during the burial ritual in a celebration of the renewal of life and the continuing abundance of the earth.

The force of the creative instinct in every facet of life is seen again in the handiwork of the carved coffins, each individually designed in the pattern and style of the tribal and individual emblems. The placement of the encoffined corpses in the cool underground caves has the effect of preserving the flesh of the dead, just as the mummified corpses of the Pharaohs preserved them from the ravages of time, deep in the recesses of the pyramids. But there is no corresponding sense of the individual's isolation here; the coffins are stacked high to the ceilings of the caves, filling the cool inner chambers, and spilling out from the cave's entrance.

The manifest dignity of this highly personalized treatment of death and the immortality of the tribe deserves our utmost respect, and compels us to view these burial rites just as they do with uplifted spirits, creative energy and total immersion in the eternal present.

The tribes are rapidly approaching cultural extinction-the present generation of tribal elders has seen its children and grandchildren turn from the old ways and increasingly adopt modern dress and customs. This decline has occurred within the space of just four or five decades, so that a single family of three generations may comprise a lone headhunting elder, his semi-civilized son, and a Western-dressed Christian teenage grandson.

The photographs presented in this book represent the last generation of Filipino headhunters, people with customs and concerns very alien to those of urbanized Westerners. The childlike simplicity of these tribespeople should never be confused with any lack of artistic sophistication or absence of moral integrity. Those condemning the allegedly barbaric act of headhunting might want to reconsider the role of their own modern culture in exterminating the primitive and natural world that has nurtured it.

The extinction of the headhunters will mark the end of a deeply spiritual, cohesive social structure, the tribe and the village, where respect for nature and life are paramount. In this world without walls, our artificial barriers between individuals, families and nations never arise; the individual interacts freely and instinctively with everyone in the surrounding world. Comparing their world and ours, one might well conclude that the newfound doctrine of cultural relativism is mistaken; its attributes far too much dignity and equality to our own very technologically advanced but morally reprehensible modern culture.

In spite of the ongoing destruction of a way of life, we may take some consolation from their deeply-felt belief in their tribal and personal immortality. The traditions and folkways of the Filipino headhunters may well die out, at least in the narrow, Western sense of lost villages, tribes and peoples. But the core values and aesthetics of the primitive world will live on within us, long after the last headhunter is gone from the Philippine mountains. The greatest loss, indeed, will be to our understanding of ourselves and our most primordial instinct; the instinct for the integration of life, death and love into the art of living...

COMMON TRIBAL WORDS

The following list offers translations of commonly used Bontoc, Ifugao, and Kalinga words. Each region, however, has its own distinct variations on the language of the province, and vocabulary frequently differs from one village to another.

agawen-- basket carried into rice paddies for collecting snails (Bontoc)
ai-in-- woman's dress [var. of Ifugao/Bontoc tapis] (Kalinga)
alongan-- coffin (Bontoc)
angan-- sleeping area in the women's dormitory (Bontoc)
anito-- sculpted human head used to mark boundaries (Bontoc)
a-ro-- rice serving implement (Kalinga)
ato-- outdoor meeting place of the tribal elders, where the men sit and debate tribal affairs (Bontoc).
Baki-- name of the principal religion (Ifugao)
bangi-bang-- headhunting ritual (Bontoc)
balalka-- man's circular hat for storage of valuables (Bontoc)
bayaong-- Mombaki shaman's blanket (Ifugao)
bayo-- ritual dance (Ifugao)
benale-- conical basket used to store large quantities of rice (Bontoc)
binohilen-- man's loincloth (Ifugao)
boaya-- headhunter's necklace of bones, shells or teeth (Bontoc)
bolo-- machete (Bontoc/Ifugao)
bopong-- peace pact (Kalinga)
Bugan-- goddess, wife of Lenchao (Batad Village, Ifugao)
bulul-- carved wooden rice protector idol (Ifugao)
butung-- man's bag with brass coil handle (Ifugao)
canao -- ritual healing sacrifice (Ifugao)
chak-lang -- headhunter's chest tattoo [var. of Kalinga fatoc] (Bontoc)
choksu-- utility work bench in the communal hut (Bontoc)
daya-- god who brings life and death (Ifugao)
dap-ay-- communal hut used for rituals and ceremonies (Bontoc)
dinalo-- star-shaped bowl used to serve rice wine in rituals (Ifugao)
dyato-- ritual to assist fermentation of rice wine (Ifugao)
dadawak-- courtship ritual of visits and gift-giving (Bontoc)
dalolos-- circular plate for carving and serving meet at rituals (Bontoc)
echaw-- bird listened for in ritual done before headhunting (Kalinga)
falos-- headhunting ritual (Kalinga)
fa-ar-- man's loin-cloth (Kalinga)
fa-og-- headhunting breaking the peace pact (Kalinga)
fang-fanga-- tobacco pipe (Kalinga)
fatoc-- decorative body tattoos of men or women (Kalinga)
fatto-ag-- human skull (Kalinga)
focus-- woven rattan storage baskets (Kalinga)
fongor-- glass or plastic beads worn by women (Kalinga)
foronit-- headhunting battle (Kalinga)
gaklab-- miniature ritual shield (Bontoc)
gansa-- gong handle (Ifugao)
hagabi-- ritual bench (Ifugao)
hackalong-- ladle (Ifugao)
hipag-- small bulul placed in punam han offertory box as part of a sacrifice (Ifugao)
iggaksias kallingang-- "I will cut your head so you will rest in peace" (Kalinga saying)
Kabunian-- ultimate spiritual power or god (Kalinga)
kadangyan-- nobleman (Ifugao)
kalasag-- shield (Bontoc)
kaman-- headhunter's curved ax (Bontoc)
kindoman-- pipe for smoking (Ifugao)
lalo-- ritual dance performed prior to headhunting (Kalinga)
Lenchao-- male god, husband of Bugan (Batad Village, Ifugao)
li-im-- working/eating area of the communal hut (Bontoc)
linglingo-- earring or necklace fertility charm (Bontoc/Ifugao)
ludi-- mortar for crushing foods (Ifugao)
lufay-- earring or pendant fertility symbol [var. of Bontoc/Ifugao linglingo] (Kalinga)
Macnoman-- ultimate spiritual power or god (Batad village, Ifugao)
machongal-- ritual listening for birds before headhunting (Kalinga)
mamar-- ritual dance performed after headhunting (Kalinga)
mandadawak-- priest or shaman who conducts rituals (Kalinga)
mombaki-- priest or shaman who conducts rituals (Ifugao)
mom batak-- harvest ritual (Ifugao)
ocali-- names of rituals (Kalinga)
o-kong-- man's hat [var. of Bontoc socyop] (Kalinga)
olifao-- metal mouth-harp with bamboo sheath (Kalinga)
padao-- wooden idol, sometimes with pointed end stuck in ground (Ifugao and Bontoc)
pango -- women's decorative tattoos [var. Kalinga fatoc] (Bontoc)
papitian-- harvest ritual (Kalinga)

LEXICON

pagata bodong-- peace pact rules (Kalinga)
pili-- protective god (Ifugao)
pinagas-- headhunting ax [var. of Bontoc kaman] (Kalinga)
pinangpanga-- man's fertility pendant [var. Ifugao linglingo (Bontoc)
pinaoo-- food serving ladle (Kalinga)
pangapang-- boar tusk necklace for males (Ifugao)
punam han-- sacrificial box used to assure health, a good harvest, or fermentation of rice wine (Ifugao)
sanggi-- ritual gong handle (Kalinga)
socyop-- man's round woven straw hat (Bontoc)
soklut-- cooking area of the communal hut (Bontoc)
tacyad-- woman's woven textile belt (Kalinga)
tapis-- women's dress (Bontoc and Ifugao)
tap-an-- rice pounding surface in the communal hut (Bontoc)
tapuy-- rice wine (Ifugao)
tongkil-- headhunter's ritual arm band (Bontoc)
tinganatago-- household deity figure [var. of Ifugao bulul] (Bontoc)
tobi-- spear (Kalinga)
topil--small square basket used to carry lunch meal (Bontoc)
tuckar-- headhunter's ritual arm band (Kalinga)
tufay-- headhunter's spear (Bontoc)
ulog-- dormitory house for girls and unmarried young women (Bontoc)

BIBLIOGRAPHY

Barton, Roy Franklin. The Halfway Sun: Life Among the Head-Hunters of the Philippines. New York: Brewer and Warren, 1930.

Barton, Roy Franklin. The Kalingas: Their Institutions and Custom Law. Chicago: University of Chicago Press, 1949.

Botengan, Kate. Bontoc Life Ways: A Study in Education and Culture. Manila: Centro Escolar University Research and Development Center, 1976.

Casino, Eric. Ethnographic Art of the Philippines. Manila, 1973.

Cawed, Carmencita Oteysa. The Culture of the Bontoc Igorot. Manila: M.C.S., 1972.

Curtis, Edward S. In the Land of the Head Hunters. Berkeley, California: Ten Speed Press, 1992.

DeRaedt, Jules. Kalinga Sacrifice. Baguio City, Philippines: Cordillera Studies Center, University of the Philippines College Baguio, June 1989. (Cordillera Monography No. 4)

Dozier, Edward P. The Kalinga of Northern Luzon. San Francisco and New York: Holt, Rinehart and Winston, 1972.

Dozier, Edward P. Mountain Arbiters: The Changing Life of the Hill People. Tucson: University of Arizona Press, 1966.

Early, John. A Short History of the Mountain Province. Manila: Bureau of Public Printing, 1930.

Ellis, George. Arts and Peoples of the Northern Philippines. The People and Art of the Philippines. Los Angeles: Museum of Cultural History, UCLA, 1981

Jenks, Albert E. The Bontoc Igorot. Manila: Bureau of Public Printing, 1905.

Kane, Samuel. Thirty Years Among the Philippine Head-Hunters. New York: Grosset and Dunlop, 1933.

Keesing, Felix. Taming Philippine Headhunters: A Case Study of Government and Cultural Change in Northern Luzon. Palo Alto, California: Stanford University Press, 1933.

Longacre, William A., and Skibo, James M. Kalinga Ethnoarchaeology: Expanding Archaeological Method and Theory. Washington, D.C.: Smithsonian, 1994.

Mayuga, Sylvia, and Yuson, Alfred. The Philippines. Hong Kong: APA Productions, 1987.

Monpaot: Cordillera Functional Sculptures. Manila: Sentrong Pangkultura Ng Pilipinas (Cultural Center of the Philippines),1992.

Nance, John. The Gentle Tasaday: A Stone Age People in the Philippine Rain Forest. New York: Harcourt Brace Jovanovich,1975.

Pain, Francis. The Making of Kalinga Pagta/Bodoonog, 1994

Palencia, Joaquin. The Ifugao Bulul and Its Regional Styles. Arts in Asia, November-December 1989, pp. 142.-147.

"The Philippines." Europa World Yearbook 1994. London: Europa, 1994. Vol. II, p. 2378.

Prill-Brett, June. Pechen: The Bontok Peace Pact Institution. Baguio City, Philippines: Cordillera Studies Center, University of the Philippines College Baguio, May 1987. (Cordillera Monograph 1).

Rosalda, Renato. Ilogot Headhunters, 1883-1974: A Study in Society and History. Palo Alto, California: Stanford University Press, 1980.

Roxas-Lim, Aurora. "Art in Ifugao Society." Asian Studies, Vol. XI, No. 2, (August 1973), p. 3.

Russell, Susan D., and Cunningham, Clark E. Changing Lives, Changing Rites: Ritual & Social Dynamics in the Philippine and Indonesian Uplands. Ann Arbor: University of Michigan Press,1989.

Scott, William Henry. "Cordillera Architecture in Northern Luzon."Folklore Studies, Vol. 21 (1962).

Scott, William Henry. On the Cordilleras: A Look at the People and Cultures of the Mountain Province. Manila: M.C.S., 1966.

Wilson, Laurence. The Skyland of the Philippines. Manila: Benipayo Press, 1956.

Worcester, Dean. "Headhunters of Northern Luzon." National Geographic, Vol. 23, No. 9 (September 1912)